WHITHER O SHIP

STANLEY ROGER GREEN

Whither O Ship

Adventures in a Tramp Steamer

PETER OWEN · LONDON

ISBN 0 7206 0743 4

The publishers acknowledge subsidy
from the Scottish Arts Council towards
the publication of this volume.

PETER OWEN PUBLISHERS
73 Kenway Road London SW5 0RE

First published in Great Britain 1989
© Stanley Roger Green 1989

Printed in Great Britain by Billings of Worcester

Whither, O splendid ship, thy white sails crowding,
Leaning across the bosom of the urgent West,
That fearest nor sea rising, nor sky clouding,
Whither away, fair rover, and what thy quest?

Robert Bridges, 'A Passer-by'

CONTENTS

The proper names and nicknames, given to the characters who appear in this book, have been fictionalized for reasons of tact or an imperfect memory.

S.R.G.

Prologue

It may have been while I was sorting out the papers of a recently dead uncle that the seed of this story took root; for I discovered in the mass of accumulated documents, diaries and memorabilia of a long life, spent mainly as a physician, that late in his career he had dropped everything and more or less run away to sea – as a ship's doctor. It was the first I had heard of it, but I should not have been surprised: the sea has flowed, as it were, through the family veins for generations, on both sides. Some kinsmen, like my uncle, had yielded to a sudden compulsion to quit a safe routine and go seafaring for a few years, to get it out of their system before settling down. Others had made it their career, like my father; and my great-grandfather who had been master of a windjammer in the last century. A hard man by all accounts, but ship's captains who were not harsh disciplinarians never survived for long against the cutthroats and desperadoes who made up the crews in the days of sail. Evidently his more gentle natured son thought so, for he abandoned the nautical life after only two trips on a sailing-ship as a cadet. In this respect my own spell at sea resembled my grandfather's, although our circumstances could not have been more different.

Then not long ago as I was wandering about Leith docks and noticing how ungainly and charmless were the vessels lining the quays, and how devoid they were of any romantic resonance, it struck me that there had been as many changes wrought in shipping between my grandfather's period and my own time at sea, as between the latter and the present day.

The seed grew and shot forth leaves: I would try to recapture as faithfully as memory would allow those scenes and events of forty years ago when I circled the globe on a tramp steamer. In the history of maritime travel there was never a period quite like it. It will never happen again.

This then is a personal record of that time, and if any former shipmates of mine should read these pages they may recall those days with relish, and perhaps judge my depiction of them with charity. They will notice, however, that for reasons of narrative convenience and dramatic continuity, I have fused the two trips I made in the SS *Rembrandt* into one. But in fact it is a tale of two voyages after all, for almost as soon as I had set sail, I guessed I had embarked on a different kind of journey altogether, an internal voyage of discovery that became truly apparent only when I had read the finished story.

I should explain that I did not at first set off with my father's blessing, and that it was only after months of pleading that I was permitted to leave school and enrol at Leith Nautical College, there to prepare for the second mate's certificate examination. This was taken after an obligatory apprenticeship of four years at sea, and for that to happen it was necessary to be indentured by a shipping company.

At the end of the college course some of us took a forestry job in the Borders while we waited for replies to our applications. I was alone in the camp bothy when the cook came in and handed me a telegram. It read like a fanfare: REPORT TO SS REMBRANDT ALBERT DOCK LIVERPOOL.

Father had relented. The telegram came from a company he had sailed with for some years.

1

The SS *Rembrandt*

The days are sick and cold, and the skies are grey and old,
  And the twice-breathed airs blow damp;
And I'd sell my tired soul for the bucking beam-sea roll
  Of a black Bilbao tramp;
  With her load-line over her hatch, dear lass,
  And a drunken dago crew,
  And her nose held down on the old trail,
  our own trail, the out trail
  From Cadiz Bar on the Long Trail – the trail
  that is always new.

  Rudyard Kipling, 'The Long Trail'

A few weeks later I was trudging the quaysides in search of my ship. It was late summer but chill rain was falling, and fitful winds stirred the harbour waters with flecks of spume. The dock buildings and warehouses were drab and gaunt, and the ships lining the wharfs seemed as sullen and dejected as beaten dogs. Huge mobile cranes reared and dipped into their holds like weird mechanical horses feeding from cavernous troughs. Everywhere there was the controlled frenzy of cargo-loading, a grinding of chains and rattle of winches, the crashing of cargo trays hitting the wharfs, the cries of stevedores.

I felt dazed by the incessant racket as I picked my way through the dockside clutter, passing one after another the moored merchantmen: tramp steamers, liberty boats, victory boats, the occasional cargo passenger. All of them were painted a dull uniform grey, their hulls streaked with ordure, and all were armed fore and aft with guns, 4-inchers or 12-pounders; and on monkey islands or at the wings of the bridge were oerlikon machine-guns. I wondered if I should ever have to use any of them. My ears still ached from a gunnery course we had attended before leaving nautical college. The hideous explosions of the 4-inch gun had numbed my brain, and when it was my turn to fix the sights on the wicker target that was being towed by a trawler offshore, I almost sank the trawler. . . .

I reached the end of one dock and rather wearily set off for the next one. It was a busy scene, and glimpsed in perspective the dockside resembled a tangled forest of cranes, masts and rigging, funnels and Samson-posts. Somehow I hoped the SS *Rembrandt* would have no Samson-posts. Dropping my bags to ease aching shoulders, I looked around the entire dock, in which there was hardly a vacant berth, and told myself that these ships were the lucky ones. They had escaped Doenitz's U-boat packs, they had made it to safety. But the war in Europe was over, and I felt in some way cheated.

Then I noticed an inscription on the bows of a cargo steamer even more hangdog in appearance than the others, and my quest was at an end. The SS *Rembrandt* was no oil painting. She was a flush-decked coal-burner with five hatches and raised poop and fo'c's'le head of about 6,000 tons displacement. A tramp indeed! Truly a slattern of a ship, her function one of unmitigated drudgery. Even the armour-plating of the bridge was rusty and mottled with daubs of red lead. But she had no Samson-posts, and I picked up my bags and made for the shabby gangway amidships with a sudden elation despite a covert anxiety that had been with me since the arrival of the telegram. Apart from a weekend spent on my father's last ship when it had docked at Dundee, I had had no closer experience of merchantmen than what could be gained from library books, lectures at nautical college or implausible sea stories at the cinema.

My situation was now alarmingly real: the filthy decks, the clamorous steam winches, the esoteric activities of the steve-dores, were part of a new world in which I was a stranger despite the Articles of Indenture I had signed, which bound me to the company as an apprentice for four years. And I was acutely aware that my doeskin uniform with its high-brimmed cap, which threatened to slide over my forehead at intervals, clearly announced my inexperience to all the world.

As I mounted the gangway, I reflected that it was cold comfort to know that no seaman since the dawn of ocean travel had boarded his first ship without similar emotions. One thing was certain: when I walked down that gangway for the last time, I should be a different person. 'Whatever there is in a man, the sea will bring it out.' That ambiguous adage had been quoted by more than one seagoing relative at home. But what was it that lay coiled and dormant inside of me, that waited only on nautical influences to emerge from its hiding-place? Now I was about to find out, and the prospect of the revelation filled me with excitement and panic in equal measure.

I had dumped my bags and wandered around the decks hoping to find someone in authority when a laconic North Country voice called down from the boat deck: 'Ah said, y'doan't want t'leave y'r gear like that, cobber. Shower o' thievin' boogers around 'ere. . . .'

A stevedore directing a cargo tray into the hold looked round and sneered.

From the rolled-up, jauntily worn Balaclava and the clean denims, I guessed the man up top was one of the crew. He was renewing ropes through the sheaves of the lifeboat davits.

'You th'new cadet, like?' he asked.

'Well, I'm not Admiral Cunningham,' I replied facetiously, and retrieved my suitcases. 'Where do I find the mate?'

'Down that alleyway, pro'bly. He should be sober now. An' then again . . . maybe not.' And he gestured comically with a marlinspike. 'Yorky's me name. An' you're a Jock, right?'

I nodded and turned into the alleyway feeling marginally less of a stranger. Within minutes my rank and nationality had been identified, I had made an acquaintance, and learnt to distinguish crew from longshoremen. This was progress.

The mate was dark and rotund with lazy, intolerant eyes, and gave an impression of stolid resourcefulness. When he laughed, which was seldom, his uniformed corpulent figure shook with the effort like a black blancmange. His name was Gregan, I was told, as he showed me to my berth in the engineers' alleyway. The cabin, which I was to share with another cadet, contained two bunks with drawers, underneath, two lockers and a small table for the purposes of study. Hordes of ruddy-brown insects scurried across the bulkheads.

'You'll get used to the cockroaches,' said Mr Gregan. He made the advice sound like an order, but I never did get used to them. Long, dark grandfathers, mothers carrying eggs, tiny black offspring, all grouped and scuttled and re-formed like Rorschach tests whenever a drawer was opened or a mattress upturned. To leave half a melon untended for five minutes was to create a colony. 'The time to worry about them', the older seamen would say, 'is when you try to hang your coat on a hook and the hook moves.' But I worried about them all the time.

'Your mate, Minto, will be alongside, next week,' said Mr Gregan. 'Get settled in, and you can turn to tomorrow after breakfast. Dinner's at seven sharp.' Then he was off, imparting a faint whiff of whisky to the ambience of the cheerless room.

I opened a port, but the confused clattering sounds of the dockside surged in with a taste of gritty air, and so I closed it again. I tried not to think of the cockroaches, or how they might penetrate ears or nostrils while I was asleep.

At dinner, in the oak-veneered saloon, I met a few other officers; engineers mainly, the second mate and a junior sparks from Glasgow. They seemed amiable but taciturn as though overtaken by war weariness, except for the fourth engineer, an Ulsterman, whose mangled vowels and burred consonants tended to delay complete understanding of his cheerful loquacity.

'Green ...,' he said thoughtfully, in response to my name. 'Hey, Chief, sure you sailed wit' a Jock Green on the old *Ribera*?'

'It was the *Romney*,' broke in the sparks. 'She was torpedoed off Newfoundland.'

'An' I'm after tellin' you it was the *Ribera*. Sure it was, Chief?'

'Excuse me, Fourth,' drawled the sparks with laconic sarcasm, 'but you get to know people quite intimately when you share a lifeboat with them for four days. You see, I was there.'

The confusion was understandable. For some elegant but quirky reason it was company policy to name the ships after painters whose name began with the letter R – Reynolds, Raphael, Raeburn, and so forth. Even as the argument droned on, I was looking at an excellent print of *The Golden Helmet*; and I had noticed on the opposite bulkhead previously Hendrikje Stoeffels leaning drowsily from her bed-closet just as Rembrandt

˙ had depicted her three centuries ago. You could almost smell the bedclothes.

'You're both right,' said the chief finally. 'Jock sailed as second on the *Ribera* after the *Romney* went down.' He turned to me: 'A relation of yours maybe?'

'My father.'

'I see. . . .'

They fell silent and I knew they were surmising how I had come by my appointment. 'It's not what you know, it's who you know,' my father had declared often enough. And berths for cadets were never plentiful.

'He's a good engineer, your father,' said the chief. 'Likes a drink though.'

The fourth snorted. 'This blurry company'd drive anny maun t' the drink! You'll find out, Jock.' Thus I was rechristened.

The mate at the head of the table chortled, his bulky shoulders heaving: 'Don't disillusion the lad on his first day, Fourth. Wait till tomorrow!' And he rose to leave. The captain hadn't yet appeared.

The next morning I donned my seconds, a blue battledress, and tried to rub the sheen off the gold flashes at the lapels. I failed. Likewise my attempt to crumple the cap into a simulation of weather-beaten long service. After breakfast I reported to the mate.

'Get a longshoreman and sound the bilges,' he grunted, and waddled off before I could ask why this should be necessary in port, or indeed how it was to be done. Presumably I was meant to know these things.

I approached a knot of stevedores at the gangway with some diffidence. This would be my first given order as an officer of the Merchant Navy. It had to be delivered in such a manner that would not expose my ignorance or invite ridicule: firm enough to be responded to, but not so arrogant as to provoke hostility. I had heard about the power of dockside unions. The men happened to be waiting on their foreman to allot the day's assignments, but I didn't know that then. I drew in my breath and faced them as boldly as I could.

'Er, would one of you mind helping me to sound the bilges?'

Considered as a command, it was altogether devoid of authoritative resonance, and I expected them to turn on their heels and slouch off, as though calling my bluff.

However, one of them nodded to a wizened, gnomelike figure, who promptly capered towards me and saluted. 'At your service, sir!' he barked with a grin, and his wrinkled head craned round to exchange a not quite invisible wink with his comrades. I supposed this to mean, 'Imagine an old sweat like *me* taking orders from a kid still wet behind the ears!' And to confirm how farcical the situation was, he immediately took the initiative. 'Right, wacker. I'll get t' rod from Chippy's locker, an' you get y'r book, like. . . .'

Here was another dilemma. What kind of book did he mean? A textbook, a manual of some sort? Then light streamed in: since bilges were separated by the main bulkheads, there had to be ten of them on a ship with five holds; plus two each for the engine-room and stokehold. So my assistant's inference could be only that I was to make a record of the soundings which he would take with his rod.

When I got back from my cabin with a notebook, he had already unscrewed a brass cap in the deck and was paying a rod and line into a duct. Moments later he had drawn it up, and the gnarled face bent over the rod's end was measuring the result. 'Eight inches!' he called out.

'Eight inches,' I repeated, imagining this was the nautical thing to do, but not sure whether the figure he had quoted was cause for relief or alarm. But nothing in the man's manner suggested that we should abandon ship, so I jotted down 'eight inches' and inscribed above it *Number Three Hold, Starboard*.

I relaxed, for there was nothing to worry about. Our *modus operandi* established, we progressed round all the other rodding eyes until the survey was complete. The soundings varied little and I assumed correctly that Mr Gregan would find nothing amiss.

By lunch-time I felt myself to be one of the crew, capable of taking orders, relaying them to subordinates and ensuring their proper execution. I almost strutted into the saloon to mingle and chat with my brother officers and order courses from the white-clad stewards who busied themselves on our behalf.

A lull crept over the conversation as the captain entered, a bluff bull of a man with a red-hot face wearing a belligerent expression, which I later found to be largely assumed. His presence filled the room, and I sensed my newly won self-esteem contract to vanishing-point. Here was authority personified, leaving no doubt about who was master of the ship.

The brusque affability of his greeting drew respectful replies from the other officers, then we sat down to our places, mine at the end of one of the two tables in the room. Hendrikje gave me an enigmatic glance.

Captain Davis led the conversation, his pleasant Welsh intonation effortlessly dominating the voices of his subordinates, particularly that of the chief sparks whose BBC announcer's accents seemed effete and insincere by comparison.

'We must do something about the theft of cargo, gentlemen,' he said latterly, pushing aside his plate. 'It's coming out as fast as it goes in! I wonder if we'll ever leave port at this rate, Mr Gregan?'

'I agree, sir. It's reached epidemic proportions,' said the mate.

'But what's the cure? That's what I want to know.'

'I wish anyone knew, sir. The stevedores are well organized, and we haven't enough crew aboard to supervise them.'

'The crew? Sweepings of Liverpool gaol, most of them. They're at it, too. And the police can do nothing, so they say.'

'I've been thinking of putting the apprentices on night-watch as an experiment,' said the mate. 'It might act as a deterrent. We could start with Minto. He's due back shortly.'

The captain looked doubtful, and his fierce gaze suddenly shot in my direction. 'We'll give it a try, Mr Gregan. . . . So you are Green, I believe? The superintendent tells me you did well at nautical college. But will you do so well at the real thing, boyo?'

'I'll try, sir,' I replied.

'You had better try, sir,' he retorted, 'or I'll want to know why.' Then in a more kindly tone: 'You hail from Edinburgh, I hear. A beeootiful city, gentlemen. There's no place like it, not in England or even Wales. Our young friend will find Liverpool a strange contrast.'

'That is an understatement, sir,' I said, overcoming my nervousness too hastily. There was a chilling pause, then the captain's chesty laughter burst forth and the others joined in.

Under cover of their amusement, I visualized the contrast. Edinburgh with its hills and thorny silhouettes resembled an arthritic old aristocrat who had seen better days, while Liverpool seemed like a bustling Edwardian merchant in whom opulence and vulgarity fought for predominance. Then I remembered that Edinburgh had seemed strident and sophisticated after the years I spent in the countryside as an evacuee. A little over a year ago I had been climbing trees, swimming rivers, camping in the hills, and smearing Brylcreem on my hair in the hope of alluring the best-looking girls at school dances. Now I was in an utterly different world, and I wondered how successfully I should inhabit it. One glance at the seasoned, experienced faces of my senior officers convinced me that I was ignorant of more things than navigation and practical seamanship.

'D'you know the Black Bull?' the fourth engineer asked suddenly.

'No, I've never heard of it.'

'An' you come from Edinburgh? Sure, the Black Bull's famous! What about Fairley's then? You must have heard of that?'

'I'm sorry, but I haven't . . .'

The captain interrupted these nostalgic inquiries: 'It is possible, Mr Riley, that not everyone shares your enthusiasm for low drinking dens, as I deem them to be. . . . Besides, the lad's only sixteen. He may never have been to a public house. Have you, Green?'

'Once, sir, with my father . . . I had an orange juice. . . .'

The officers smiled and rose to leave. 'Just you stick to the soft drinks, son,' said the chief engineer in passing. 'Too many good men have foundered on the alternative. . . .'

I guessed he was referring to my father.

2

False Start

My curiosity about the other cadet increased as the day of his arrival drew nearer. Hints dropped in the saloon about Ralph Minto suggested he was a 'company's man' aboard yet something of a tearaway ashore. But this in itself hardly completed a picture of my opposite number in the hierarchy of the crew. So one evening I yielded to scurrilous temptation and opened his drawers in search of clues to his personality, on the dubious grounds that I had a right to know what sort of person I was to be cooped up with for two years.

The first drawer contained a sheet of paper with a stark message that leapt out like a rodent from a burrow: *Nosy Bugger!* I banged the drawer shut and, more cautiously, opened the adjoining one. A studio portrait of a dark, lovely girl wearing a mantilla smiled up at me. Across an ornate fan she was holding were the words *To my darling Ralph – Ever yours, Dorothy.* Which didn't sound very Spanish, but her existence provided an obscure justification for my inquisitiveness, and I searched no more.

By then I had become acquainted with some of the men down aft, mainly through distributing mail each morning, a pleasant task that helped to lower social barriers, at least among the deck crew. The firemen and trimmers were more reserved and tended to slouch along the deck hardly taking their eyes from it while chewing a corner of the obligatory sweat-rag which was worn round the neck. And some of the stokehold gang adopted a hostile silence in my presence which reminded me of the captain's remark about 'the sweepings of Liverpool gaol'. Some months later, I stoked up a furnace for half an hour – 'put a pitch

on' – and discovered how agonizingly laborious a stoker's work
can be. The heat was appalling, and I understood then why
their heels dragged after a four-hour watch.

The deck seaman were breezier and more alert, fond of jokes
with nautical allusions, took a pride in their appearance even in
working clothes, and usually were of a sunnier disposition than
their counterparts below. But there were two notable excep-
tions. 'Chippy' the carpenter, and the bosun, were elderly men
by Merchant Navy standards. Both had gone to sea under sail
originally, and forty years of foreign climates had sculpted their
grizzled heads into a cross between gargoyles and Red Indian
chiefs. Their rare remarks were uttered with pessimistic irony,
and their manner gave an impression of disdain for the
effeminacy of steam propulsion and its debilitating effects on
contemporary seamen. 'When I first went to sea,' Chippy would
say occasionally, clay pipe jutting from his battered face and one
foot on a bollard as though posing for a portrait of an old salt,
'there were wooden ships and iron men. Now it's the other way
round. . . .' The younger seamen would grin mischievously and
try to look apologetic. 'Oh, you're right there, Chippy. Too
true,' they said.

At length Minto arrived, a handsome eighteen-year-old who
had sailed to many countries already and had survived the
Atlantic convoys from Loch Ewe during the second wave of
U-boat predations. He had a crisp style of conversation that
matched his pleasantly chiselled features.

'Have you met the Old Man yet?' he asked when we were
alone.

'Captain Davis? Yes.'

'A two-bottle-a-day man. Keep out of his way.'

'Two bottles of what?'

His steady gaze faltered. 'Well, not Coca Cola,' he said, and I
could see he was wondering if I were being disingenuous or if I
was just plain stupid. But I merely sought information. I had
supposed that deck officers might drink only rum, and told him
so.

He laughed. 'They wouldn't teach you much about these
things at nautical college, would they? . . . I came up through the
hawse-pipe myself.'

I wasn't sure whether this was a boast or an apology so I
changed the subject.

'The mate said he was putting us on night-watch duty, turn about.'

'He what! . . .' Minto fumed for several minutes. 'That's typical of this stinking company . . . cheapskates . . . bastards. . . . As soon as I get my ticket, I'm off!'

'What sort of . . . stinking company is it?' I asked, feeling suddenly depressed.

'They work a cheap labour racket with the apprentices, that's what. So we turn to with the men, except we get the shitty jobs, having no union to protect us. Such as night-watchman. And topping up the tank on monkey island. Have they got you on that yet?'

'No.'

'They will,' said Minto.

And they did, the very next day. Between the fiddley and the galley door a pump handle was fixed to the bulkhead, and by manipulating this I pumped water to a cistern above the deck officers' quarters until my arms were paralysed with fatigue and my ears throbbed with the monotonous clanking. The gnomelike stevedore was working the winch at number three hatch with expert aplomb, and that too added to the din. Huge bombs were being shipped aboard.

'What's a' do there, wacker!' called out the stevedore who had a clear view of my activity.

I was too breathless to reply, but it seemed to me his sidelong smile conveyed a smug satisfaction that our roles had become subtly reversed. Now I was in the inferior position, a ship's menial: if not a hewer of wood, certainly a drawer of water. Anyone could do my job, but no one would have entrusted me with the task of lowering enormous bombs into the hold, which my former subordinate was accomplishing with nonchalant precision.

To take my mind of my chagrin and aching muscles I recited as many Articles of the Regulations as I could remember. All intending mates mush achieve the feat of committing thirty-eight of these to memory, word for word: 'Article One. The Rules concerning lights shall be complied with in all weathers from sunset to sunrise . . .'

'Jock! . . .'

' . . . and during such time no other lights which may be . . .'

'Hey, wacker! . . .'

' . . . mistaken for the prescribed lights shall be exhibited . . .'

'For God's sake, Green! Stop that damn' pumping, will you!'

I looked up then, and it was apparent that I had topped up the tank only too well. The mate, and a ship's chandler whom I had met at lunch, had left the captain's suite on the boat-deck just in time to be deluged by a watery jet from an overflow pipe. They did not appear to be happy men, especially the chandler, who had been wearing a light fawn overcoat. When their indignant bellows had eased off, I shouted up: 'How was I to know when the tank would be full?'

Yorky sidled up then, for it was he who had tried to warn me.

'Steady on, Jock. Y'don't want to rile those boogers. Cadets c'n do nowt right in Gregan's eyes, you'll see. . . .'

The mate neither looked at me nor deigned to reply to my reasonable query, and he stomped down the companionway with the chandler in a fine huff. But the stevedore, who had got a share of the spray, wrinkled his face engagingly. 'Thanks for the shower, wacker! Cooled me down, like,' he said.

Yorky and I looked down into the hold where the bombs were ranged in rows on the floor. They looked evil.

'Where do you think these are intended for, Yorky?' I asked.

'Far East, pro'bly. I only hope they've removed the detonators, that's all!'

'But if the ship caught fire or if we were shelled, they'd still blow up?'

'Oh, yes, mate. They'd still blow up, an' us wi' them. If we ever leave Liverpool, that's to say.'

Yorky's pessimism on this last point seemed justified; but despite the plunderings of the heterogeneous cargo by crew and stevedores, a day dawned when the last cargo tray was returned ashore, derricks housed and made fast, and the last hatch battened down. The Blue Peter was hoisted to the yard, the Red Ensign struck out aft, and back-lines and moorings cast off. The ship's whistle sounded a deep-throated growl of farewell and with the aid of a tug we were towed into the Mersey.

The weeks we spent in port had seemed unreal and not at all *nautical*, and yet I found the fact difficult to grasp that we had actually set sail. It was as though it were happening to someone else, an *alter ego* perhaps, with whom I must hurry to catch up if I were to make sense of it all. Yet there was no doubt of the decks' vibrating to the triple-expanding engines, of the hoot

from the departing tug and the thrilling sway of the waves as
they lunged in from the Irish Sea. And that was certainly the
Royal Liver Building receding astern behind a chorus of gulls;
and there was Birkenhead on the port bow, soon to drop back
into grey featureless distance. Then Wallasey and Bootle to
starboard until they too disappeared abaft the spreading wake.
Only when the ship rounded Holyhead on a southerly course
and a deep swell struck us beam on, inducing a profound
uneasiness in my stomach, was I convinced that it was
happening to me. Nautical college was behind me, and my
family and friends. At an age when contemporaries were
preparing for exams, playing fieldgames or tennis, going to
dances and meeting girls, I was sailing as cadet on a tramp
steamer hull down with a mixed cargo which included bombs,
and manned by a crew partly made up of the sweepings of
Liverpool gaol. And we were bound on a southerly course for
far-off lands. My feelings, therefore, were as mixed as our cargo.
But to which country we were bound for, no one could even
guess, and word hadn't filtered through from the galley, which
was the ship's equivalent of Delphi, the cook its oracle.

At smoko, as we sat on the hatch outside the pantry, the chief
steward supported Yorky's theory; that because of the bombs,
we could expect a trip to India at the least. His opinion was
taken seriously, since he knew better than anyone the quantity
of stores that had been taken on board.

At the thought of India, my mind took wing. *And after India,
maybe Hong Kong or Australia or the South Pacific....* I summoned
up pictures of blue sugar-loaf mountains looming mistily above
coral strands, canoes filled with chanting Polynesians speeding
towards our ship like a flight of arrows!

'We'll know by tomorrow, when the skipper opens his
orders,' said Chippy guardedly. He was the only man aboard to
use the term 'skipper', a relic of his days under sail. But it was
true what he said: wartime conditions still prevailed and sailing
orders were secret until a vessel was twenty-four hours out from
port.

But revelations from bridge or galley were not required. After
a day's sailing, and ten knots in a following wind seemed to be
the *Rembrandt*'s maximum speed, we watched with dismay the
bows swing round to port as she passed St David's Head and
butted into the mouth of the Bristol Channel. And at that

moment the coasts of Devon and South Wales did remind me of open jaws waiting to swallow us just as escape from the austerities of war-fatigued Britain had seemed a reality. Visions of the Orient faded from my expectations. But worse was to follow when we tied up that evening in the harbour of the prosaic town of Newport, Monmouthshire.

3

Departure

Minto had done his stint as night-watchman at Liverpool. Now it was my turn, and Mr Gregan issued instructions with characteristic brevity. 'And keep a sharp watch on number one and five holds. The ship's got booze aboard,' he concluded and ambled back to the saloon.

And not only the ship, I thought, watching his bulk blot out the light from the alleyway as he heaved a fat leg over the coaming. I had been up and doing since dawn, but that aspect of things hadn't been discussed; nor that I should be in a lethargic condition from midnight onwards. What mattered was that I was to prevent, in a manner unspecified, drink-crazed felons from pilfering cargo. His inference that holds amidships were too close to the officers' quarters to need supervision, hardly lessened my anxiety.

For the first few nights all went well. As instructed, I checked the rat-guards and the lights, adjusted the gangway in relation to the quayside as the tide rose and fell, helped drunken seamen aboard, hauled down the flag at sunset, and periodically toured the hatches, where everything was as quiet as a graveyard. The only sounds were the lapping of the black waters against the hull and the rattle of the lamp above the gangway as it swayed in the wind. It was pleasant to return to the warm galley and con up on the Articles over a mug of cocoa.

Another task was to keep the galley stove alight, both for heat and to cook the enormous unrationed meals which I shared with Bill the donkeyman, also on night duty. His curious title derived from his responsibility for tending the donkey boiler which supplied hot water in port. Bill was a genial, generous-hearted

man and his company did much to relieve the tedium of my
vigils. On rare occasions he would recount his experiences; of
being torpedoed, the huge cataract of sea flooding the engine-
room; of days spent in open boats without food or water; and
finally, his being picked up by a German destroyer and interned
in France, where food was almost as scarce as in the lifeboats.
And all this he would relate with a grin and a shrug, as though
to say: Despite what life threw at me, I'm still here to joke about
it, and that can't be bad. Yet his stories reminded me yet again
that I had been deprived of the chance of heroic action, of
hardship and danger on the high seas. The war was still going
on in Japan but it was too remote to be imaginable; nor could I
see myself providing an effective opposition by means of the
oerlikons against a kamikaze pilot. One would simply have to
wait for the crash. Heroism would be superfluous.

So much for the influence of wartime naval films. I was
equally credulous at more mundane levels. One night I was
sitting on the galley table reading Nicholls's *Seamanship and
Nautical Knowledge* when a fireman came in, ostensibly for hot
water. 'Ah heard ye were fae Emburgh,' he burred in thick
Clydeside accents as he spurted water from the urn into his jug.
'Emburgh is the capital, but Glesga *has* the capital, eh, Mac?'
Then without waiting for a reply to this *aperçu*, he said: 'Ach,
nae haurd feelins. Us Jocks maun stick th'gither, ken?'

'Why?' I asked. 'Is there a conspiracy against us?'

That was all he needed: 'Whit? No hauf. See they Sassenachs. . . .' And he was off on a droll tirade against our southern
neighbours. His water cooled in the jug but the guttural
eloquence flowed on. At one point I heard some men outside,
apparently in high good humour, and assuming they were crew
returning from the pubs of Newport I didn't investigate. Soon
all was quiet again and, eventually, so was my garrulous fellow
Scot.

'Ah've enjoyed our natter, Mac,' said the fireman, though he
had done all the talking. 'Whit aboot comin' doon aft an' meetin'
the lads?'

'No thanks. I'm supposed to be on watch.'

'Come on . . . y're no' wan o' they Emburgh snoabs, are ye?'

I thought about it. On a ship in which cadets acted as
night-watchman, filled water cisterns and worked alongside the
deck crew, aloofness would seem to be incongruous.

'Maybe I could take a turn down aft and drop in for a minute.'

'That's the stuff, Mac. They treat cadets like dirt on tubs like this. Gi'e yoursel' a break!' And he picked up his jug, evidently indifferent to the temperature of the contents, and led the way down aft.

The hatches were quiet, but as we passed a companion-light over the fireman's quarters, a wave of song and laughter issued forth.

'Aye, they're in great form the nicht!' said my guide and motioned me to follow him down the steps to the mess.

The place was filled with firemen and trimmers mainly, but I recognized a few of the deck squad through the billowing fug. All of them were drinking cans of beer at some speed and replacing them regularly from cartons on the table.

'Hey, youse! Meet the new cadet. He's a braw lad fae the second best toon in Sco'land,' said my companion.

The response was amiable and I was passed a can. I didn't much care for the taste of beer but I thought it prudent to pretend I was used to the stuff.

'They're a great bunch o' mates,' confided the fireman in my ear as he placed another opened can at my side.

'I thought you didn't like Sassenachs?' I whispered back.

'Ach, we're a' Jock Tamson's bairns, suir we are . . .'

'Ah say, Jock! What about a song, then?' The invitation, which was greeted by all hands with enthusiasm, came from a small, grinning Welshman known as Jonesy.

'But I can't sing a note,' I said truthfully.

'Come on, Jock! Give us "Bonnie Mary o' Argyle" for starters!' This suggestion was made by Yorky and lustily endorsed by the company, Jonesy volunteering to help out with such words as he could remember.

'All right,' I agreed at last, thinking that it would provide an opportunity for a diplomatic departure. 'And then I'll have to get back on my rounds, though.'

I was dimly aware then that two men left the room.

'Oh, sure, Jock. But first, 'ave another drink.' A third can was placed in my hand. 'Now, y'can let rip, just loosen up y'r tonsils like.'

I took his advice and found that my usually uncertain tenor had developed a surprising degree of confidence, so that when I reached the song's triumphant conclusion I was beginning to

enjoy myself. But I knew I must leave, for my head was
beginning to ache; so, with the name of Burns's sweetheart of
the moment still ringing round the mess-room, I made by
escape under cover of their applause, and hardly noticed the
two men waiting at the top of the companionway with cartons
in their arms.

I stood at the taffrail for a moment, gulping the night air deep
into my lungs, then I did a complete tour of the decks to clear
my head before turning into the galley. I had visitors, and Mr
Gregan and the chief steward gave the impression that they had
been waiting for some time.

'Green! Where the hell have you been?'

'Oh, doing the rounds. Nothing to report, however.'

'Is that so? Well, I have something to report. Follow me. . . .'

At a brisk pace, we headed for the mates' alleyway and came
to a halt outside the locker-room, where the ship's supply of
liquor was kept. Or had been until recently, for the door panels
were smashed in and the place was almost empty, certainly
enough to delight a temperance society. A few ruined crates lay
around, and a carton with a trade name that looked familiar.

'So what's your explanation?' panted Mr Gregan, his adipose
tissue all aquiver. The chief steward, a man prematurely lined
by an obscure sorrow, was no less furious. As I stood between
them I felt like a prisoner under escort, and a guilty one at that.
But any explanation I could give would implicate myself as well
as the men still whooping it up and loosening their tonsils down
aft. And one did not clype. I was sure that tell-tales were no
more popular at sea than at school.

'I'm sorry, but I heard nothing,' I said, feeling my way
gingerly into this new quandary. Then I thought of a way out.
'But you did tell me to keep a close watch on number one and
five holds . . . I can't be everywhere at once, can I?'

'How the blazes can you watch out for cargo thieves when
you can't even prevent a raid on the liquor store?' roared the
mate. But the question, though relevant, was rhetorical, and
with a disgusted gesture he signalled my dismissal.

The question was interesting in several ways. Obviously I
should have to be suspicious of anyone who wanted a
prolonged conversation with me in the galley in future; and
when seamen came aboard, I should have to make sure they did
not return to their quarters via locker-rooms amidships. But no

one had explained just what I was supposed to do if I intercepted thieves, particularly if the mates were ashore at the time. And because of a lack of definition of my role, I was too unsure of myself to ask.

A few nights later I was to learn some of these things for myself.

At about two in the morning, when supper was over and the donkeyman had gone below, I made a tour of the hatches. The night was cold, but the sky was clear and I could make out the faint crests of the hills above Newport. By day they had reminded me of the Fifeshire hills as seen across the Forth from Leith. All was quiet for'ard, but as I drew level with number four hatch I noticed that the tarpaulin of the adjacent hold was disturbed. A man was leaning on the deck-rail nearby, apparently contemplating the lights of town across the harbour.

What should I do? If there was an innocent explanation, the mate would not be overjoyed at being dragged from his bunk at this hour. And desperately I wanted to believe that some careless stevedore had made a botch of covering the hatch that evening, and that the man at the rail was an insomniac or pining for some girl he had met in Newport.

If, however, the cargo were being plundered, it was a police matter; but the ship carried no telephone, and the long quays were deserted and theatrical-looking under the dock lamps.

A despicable notion occurred to me: I could tiptoe back to the galley and forget the whole incident. It was pretty certain that Minto would have done just that, and he was by no means a cowardly sort of person. And what difference would it make if there were a few more erroneous entries in the bills of lading when so much had been stolen already? Moreover, I was not very large.

Yet my rationalizations were in vain, and I found myself crossing the deck between the hatches towards the contemplative crewmen at the rail as though I were sleep-walking.

He stirred at my approach and said in feigned surprise: 'Hullo, there! Young Jock, isn't it?'

It was Waddington, a burly ordinary seaman, one of the songsters of the firemen's mess-room.

I lifted the loose tarpaulin. 'Why is the hatch open, Waddington?' I asked.

'What hatch? . . . Oh, that one! Don't know, Jock.' He paused, then: 'Oh, you don't want to go poking around there, mate,' he said, for I was peering into the gloom of the hold. I heard something move. There was a grunt and a muted curse.

'Is anyone down there?' I called out. There was an uneasy silence, so I tried a second time: 'Because if there is, you'd better come up or I'll have to get the mate along.'

But there wouldn't have been time to get anyone along, for three men rose to the hatch opening as though shot up by a geyser, and I was grabbed and lifted bodily to the deck-rail. Pausing only to change their grip from arms to ankles, they swung me out over the side and the stars above the black hills suddenly swooped up and I was staring into oily harbour waters. The peaceful hills of Cleish and Lomond seemed very far away just then, and I thought of rats swimming through the scum and filth towards me, red eyes and yellow teeth glinting in the darkness. Then a scuffle broke out behind me, and I guessed that others were contesting with my assailants and attempting to haul me back on board. I recognized Yorky's drawling voice.

'Belay there, Scouse! He's only a snotty-nosed kid!'

'Yeh, an' 'e'll soon be a fuckin' stiff! Get y'r hands off the bastard . . .'

'Give over, for Christ's sake, d'you want to be had up for manslaughter, like?'

'Let 'im go, mates. He's only a first-tripper, doesn't know 'is way about yet!' This appeal came from Waddington.

'It'll be his last trip an' all, if he goes on at this road!'

For what seemed an age, debating points were exchanged between the rival parties until eventually my feet were permitted to reach the deck. I stood there gasping and shaken, but still I sought a role that would justify my position in the eyes of absent critics, those remorseless observers of one's conduct from whom youth vainly attempts escape – parents, schoolfellows, teachers . . . 'I'm not frightened of you,' I said to them inaccurately, when normal breathing was possible. 'And you know you shouldn't have been down there.'

Scouse lunged at me then, his arms stretching out for my throat. 'I'll kill the little git! . . . ' But Yorky and Waddington moved rapidly and knocked him off balance so that he collided with the hatch coaming. Before he could get his wind back, Waddington seized my shoulders and thrust me in the direction of amidships with this urgent advice: 'Get up for'ard, Jock, and don't be a dead hero! They don't pay you enough for that. Go on, scarper!'

And I did, with some haste.

The mate sent for me the next morning. 'The donkeymen tells me you were in a rough-house last night. What happened?'

I gave him an account of the affair which would correspond with the version I had conveyed to Bill at breakfast. The donkeyman was bound to learn of it sooner or later, so I was obliged to mention the matter but without going into detail.

'Didn't you recognize any of them?'

'It was very dark, and they were in a hurry to. . . .' I paused.

'Well? To what?'

'To . . . dispose of me, you could say. I think they were firemen.'

'But you couldn't identify them?'

I shook my head, and reflected that never had I been manoeuvred into telling so many whoppers; but there seemed little choice. An identification parade would be composed of as many cargo thieves as potential homicides, and possibly I owed my life to some of the former. Of course these had been deck crew and already I felt some rapport with the men whose work I often shared. And I could not be sure that accused firemen would not turn King's evidence or, one way or another, inculpate my rescuers, who, there was no gainsaying, were guilty of theft. I was baffled. Such subjects had not been discussed at nautical college and I knew I should have to fill in the gaps of my education as I went along, even if that included distortions of the truth. My Sunday-school morality was about to undergo a sea-change.

'The donkeyman says he found a cosh down aft. He thinks it was meant for you. . . . You still don't want to name anyone?'

Good old Bill, I thought. So far he had taken an avuncular interest in me. Now he had become my protector. Yet despite this latest development I could only shake my head again.

'Then we'll see Captain Davis,' said the mate.

I was dog tired and I followed him wearily up the companion-way to the Old Man's suite, sensing the approach of a difficult interview.

The room was large and oak-veneered like the saloon, and combined the functions of lounge and office. The captain was writing at a corner desk, and even from there his personality filled the room. When matters had been explained, his hot eyes burned into mine for an uncomfortable minute. Then he spoke, slowly at first but with a gathering momentum until, leaving his desk and standing before me, he blasted forth his thoughts at short range like a salvo. 'The Service is desperately short of men,' he said, 'and we have to take what the Pool in its wisdom thinks fit to send us, including the very dregs of humanity.' He barked out a series of indictments on the Shipping Federation before narrowing the scope of his wrath to the present example of their idiocy. 'And you are quite sure you're not shielding anyone?'

'Yes, sir. Quite sure.' I had to stick to my story now.

'Are you equally sure you're not being intimidated?'

'Oh yes, sir. Quite sure.'

'I'm glad to hear of it. For by God, lad, if any man should threaten an officer of mine. . . .' And he crossed to a drawer, pulled out a vicious-looking revolver and waved it under my nose. 'Do you see this? I killed a man with it last trip on the high seas. Shot him dead like you would a mad dog. And believe me, boyo, I'd do it again if necessary.'

I believed him; but he did not countermand the order to use cadets as night-watchmen, which would have spared him the necessity. And for all his bluster, he hadn't explained how he intended to prevent a repetition of last night's incident. But there I underestimated Captain Davis.

I slept through the day usually, sometimes going ashore for a few hours before resuming my duties, so I had little contact with the crew at this time. At night I made the most cursory of inspections of the ship, confining myself to the galley for the most part, where I probed ever deeper into the intricacies of ship's work by means of my Nicholls. So I was hardly aware that new faces were to be seen aboard, particularly amongst the stokehold gang. Later I learnt that the captain had ordered a ship's inspection with police in attendance, and that cargo had been discovered in the sea-bags of certain of the firemen. I never saw my attackers again. Yorky and Waddington must have got rid of their share of the loot, for they remained on board.

The work of loading continued until the gangway was almost level with the quay at low tide, and a feverish impatience to be off and away was discernible in the faces of the crew and even the officers. At last the cook issued a tentative sailing date, and we relaxed. But he was mistaken, for history had intervened.

Late one afternoon all the church bells in town started ringing and all the ships in port sounded their horns or sirens in a mad caricature of orchestration. The war in the East was over, and Japan had accepted the terms of unconditional surrender. There was some talk in the saloon of an extraordinary new bomb which had precipitated the Allied victory, but information was scanty and the immediate effect of the Nipponese defeat was that our bombs were no longer required overseas. A huge adjustment of the cargo was now necessary and, to everyone's relief, the bombs were removed from the holds and deposited delicately in waiting trucks on the quayside.

The crew chafed at the delay, and I with them; but the postponement of our departure had, for me, certain compensations. In my first port of call, I had met a girl.

Minto had been checking my gear one day and noticed several important omissions. 'You can't possibly go to sea without oilskins and seaboots. It simply isn't done,' he said. In his view, this was analogous to the Horse Guards on parade at Buckingham Palace wearing lounge suits. So, having cabled home for cash, I got into my best uniform, set my cap at an angle in the style of Beatty of the Broke, and set off for town to make my purchases. This done, and directions given to the outfitter for their delivery, I was free to wander about Newport.

The day was dull and chilly, and the town was not being shown to best advantage, but then neither was I, for my cap still had a tendency to slew over one ear when I least expected it. Then, just as I was passing a shabby fairground, a sudden plump of rain forced me into the shelter of a shooting-gallery's awning. It was already occupied. A girl of perhaps a year older than I was shaking her fairish hair free from the collar of her coat, which she had used as a hood. She smiled to acknowledge our mutual plight; or maybe she was just amused at my cap, but we started chatting like old friends while the attendant stared into space and the fairground music wheezed on.

When the rain lessened, we agreed that what we needed was plenty of hot coffee, and soon we were sitting in a small café where we talked for hours while our clothes steamed in the warmth. We discussed tennis, hill walking, our families, and so forth. I thought it best not to darken the conversation with references to tyrannical captains who shot mutineers out of hand or gaolbirds who were inclined to dunk cadets in rat-infested harbours.

We met several times afterwards and our friendship ripened, while the unspoken topic of my imminent departure grew like a shadow between us. All at once the ship was loaded and ready for sea. I met her for a last time and we strolled round a city park where we exchanged addresses and promises to write. Rather shyly, she presented me with a medallion of St Christopher who, she said, was the patron saint of travellers. I knew nothing about saints and little about girls, but I thanked her and resolved to keep it as a memento of a pleasant friendship rather than as a talisman against marine disasters. Yet, despite a few close shaves and misadventures, I returned home safely, so maybe it worked.

When the hour approached, she accompanied me to the dock gates for a last farewell. After a clumsy embrace and a few moist kisses, I stood back and saluted as I had seen officers do in films at such poignant moments. Fortunately my cap was not dislodged by this courtesy, and I was able to take leave of her with my dignity intact.

We cast off in a silvery mist next morning, and nudged down the Channel on the tide: England on our port side, Wales to starboard, and the blue world right ahead. But soon I was too sleepy to care and headed for my bunk.

4

The Aviary

When I rose late in the afternoon there was a buzz of talk on deck. Men lined the port-side rails and the mates and the captain were crowded into a wing of the bridge. I saw what had drawn their attention. It was a mine, possibly detached from a field of them at the mouth of the Bristol Channel and now drifting at the will of currents and tides, discreetly menacing, a postscript to the war.

My immediate reaction was that we would be blown up just as we had finally set sail. I was told that official instructions obliged commanding officers to detonate mines where this was practicable and safe. The crew fell silent as we drew level with the object, which was the size of a small buoy and studded with spikes. The older seamen backed away from the rails as the captain appeared with a rifle, for at that range the blast would have devastated the lifeboats and most of the onlookers. He must have thought this too, for, taking careful aim, he fired a few rounds clear of the target, the bullets spurting spray from the waves. Captain Davis had complied with regulations in spirit if not to the letter, and the mine drifted towards the disappearing coastline. Its position would be reported, but it was now someone else's problem. Let the professionals clear up their own mess, seemed to be the thought in the minds of all hands.

Soon the mine was a distant speck against the coast; and the last links with war and home were severed. A long, flat mist was forming in stealthy coils around the headlands and merging with dusk until there was no land in sight. Ahead, there was nothing but the dark silhouettes of masts and rigging swaying gently to the motion of the ship against a sky of broken cloud and gathering stars. Yet there was a sense of freedom in the southerly breeze, and a hint of spiced lands and adventurous seaboards at journey's end that made the emptiness into which we were sailing seem inexpressibly alluring. Bishop's Rock to port winked through the darkness at intervals, showing ever more faintly until its light vanished astern and it was all left behind, already part of the past.

The last thing I remember that night was looking from the port above my bunk at the lights of shipping heading for the Channel, then I closed the port without clamping it, and fell asleep.

Scarcely a moment seemed to have passed when a violent jet of icy water burst the port open and washed me from my bunk. Shivering with cold, I staggered into morning sunlight in my drenched pyjamas, to find the bosun's squad hosing down.

'Serves you right!' yelled the bosun, adding unprintable things about first-trippers. The men, vigorously wielding their squeegees, grinned and joked as they cleaned the ship of dockyard grime from stem to stern. Seamen never wore pyjamas.

I soon forgot them and their remarks, stunned as I was by the beauty of the scene around me. I stood there dazed with wonder. There was hardly a wisp of cloud above and the ship was at the centre of a glittering sea of gold and turquoise. Even the *Rembrandt* had a sort of lustre as she dipped and swayed against the long Atlantic combers. Sometimes a seventh wave would fountain over the bows and fall crashing through the rigging to the decks in a scatter of dazzling foam which pained the eyes but inexplicably lifted the heart. I was silent at breakfast.

In the days to come, each morning brought a renewal of the wonder. I was delegated to the bosun's day-work squad and turned to with the seamen at five bells. The spectacle of brilliance and shadow, and the shifting colours of the sea, still filled me with profound delight. The work was hard, but that was part of the experience, like the throb of the engines and the rhythm of the ship as she ploughed steadily across the shimmering disc of dancing waves. It was as though the sea in such a mood exuded a mysterious bloom, the exhalation of a fundamental principle, of something like joy. It would be easy to attribute this feeling to the lively imagination of an impressionable first-tripper. But my vague apprehensions of this principle were given some justification when the first dolphins and porpoises appeared, for they seemed to respond to it. The deck-hands, and even Chippy and the bosun, would stop work to admire their antics. It was obvious that these playful mammals needed an audience, for they would circle the ship a few times to make sure everyone was paying attention before they began their act. Then in twos, threes, or even fours, they would perform balletic stunts in perfect unison, their lithe, dark and silver forms romping and cavorting in evident enjoyment of their prowess, an enjoyment that seemed to be confirmed by the smiles on their bottle-nosed faces.

In recent years I have seen few dolphins in subtropical waters, and those few were rarely given to acrobatics. Instead they lope half-heartedly from the waves, and their smiles, which had once suggested the possession of a delectable secret long since lost to man, now look wistful and formal as though they were in mourning. If man's modern needs were the cause of this, we have indeed tempted hubris.

Purdie, a junior sparks from Glasgow, was the type of know-all who corrected the misconceptions of others as though it were a wearisome duty imposed by a whimsical providence. This made arguing with him a kind of profanity, and he was usually allowed the last word. 'Of course, dolphins aren't really enjoying themselves,' he said flatly. 'That is a human assumption, an example of the Pathetic Fallacy. All that leaping in and out of the water is simply to rid themselves of sea-lice.'

'Then why should they do this in groups, with perfect timing?'

'Because they're gregarious and respond to a corporate instinct,' he said with a sigh. 'Like shearwaters in flight,' he said, clinching the matter.

I made no reply, but thinking of the knowing smiles and bulging foreheads of the creatures, I had my own opinion. And if the light of the eye is a measure of intelligence, dolphins were a cable-length ahead of some of our firemen. But dolphins hadn't permitted themselves to be organized into societies where brutalizing toil is necessary. No wonder they smiled.

Some hours before Cape Finisterre hove up on our port bow, a much larger creature broke surface and came butting through

white-veined waves towards Biscay, a silvery plume from its
blow-hole arcing in the breeze.

'It's a humpback!' cried the fourth engineer excitedly.

'Not really, Fourth,' advised Purdie. 'Anyone can see it's a
sperm whale. The box-shaped head is a characteristic. And
despite its huge grin, it's not enjoying itself either.'

I was to have a closer view of one of these monsters on the
homeward trip during an Atlantic gale when no one enjoyed
himself very much; but that was an age away.

For the present the weather was calm and the days grew
warmer, the ship travelling about two hundred and forty
nautical miles over the ground each day. By then our desti-
nations were known: Port Said for fuel, Palestine, then Greece;
and after that perhaps Algeria. The names of the countries
resounded in my head like music, and I thought pityingly of a
college friend in an oil tanker bound for Abadan in the Persian
Gulf – a hell-hole, from what I had learnt. I determined to crowd
my letters to him with descriptions and incidents of my travels
to compensate him for his miserable lot. For instance, I would
tell how, when the ship had sailed through the Straits of
Gibraltar and left Cap de Gata on the coast of Spain far behind,
we encountered other wildlife, of a surprising kind.

It was now late autumn and one morning we discovered our
ship had become a resting-place for flocks of migratory birds.
Overnight the SS *Rembrandt* was transformed into an aviary.
Every part of the superstructure was occupied by a different
species of bird which, with an uncanny sense of protocol, they
maintained throughout their stay. A peregrine falcon held
undisputed sway over the fo'c'sle head; egrets and other
wading birds strutted lugubriously around the boat-decks;
while down aft a swift or swallow roosted on every cabin
ventilator. The eyes of the latter were tightly closed most of the
time, and their tiny faces wore expressions of grumpiness which
intensified when anyone tried to feed them.

The identity of a dun-coloured bird, larger than a thrush,
which had chosen the poop-deck as its territory, caused
frequent argument. 'It's a cuckoo, sure it is,' declared the fourth
engineer.

Purdie gave a glance indicating that the only thing aboard
close to that description was the fourth engineer, and repeated
his assertion that the bird was a nightingale. Since none of the

crew had seen either bird at close quarters, and since the solitary occupant of the poop-deck never once opened its beak to confirm its identity, the argument remained irresolute.

Then one morning they were gone. Refreshed from their sojourn, they had taken off in the night, perhaps using the stars to guide them on their way, and the ship seemed a lonelier place with their passing.

But one bird did not resume the flight to warmer climes. A trimmer, coming off a gruelling watch, had thrown a hatch wedge at a wading bird as it dithered around number three hatch, as was its habit. I don't think he meant to hit it, but he did. The bird have a squawk, keeled over and fell limp. It was tossed overboard. Maybe the trimmer's act was an expression of his exhaustion, or even envy, but it was a long time before his shipmates forgave him.

If the act was brutal, the man was not; nor were many of the crew violent towards each other, at least not physically. But the old bosun, one Daly from Sunderland whom the crew were quick to dub 'Dasher', employed an aggressive turn of phrase and a withering mastery of sarcasm which made us suppose that he regretted the abolition of the rope's end, if not keel-hauling. For the first few months at sea much of his sarcasm was directed at me, and with some reason. I soon discovered that I lacked all sense of practical aptitude. My knots invariably worked loose; I coiled hawsers anticlockwise almost instinctively instead of by the seamanlike 'sunrise-to-sunset' method. Sometimes I would attempt to slip bolts into cleats from the wrong end, and I would fix rat-guards to mooring-lines reversely. All of which drew wrathful responses from Dasher Daly in a voice that sounded like the rattle of the anchor cable emerging from the hawse-pipe. Surveying the rat-guards, he growled thunderously, 'D'ye want to invite the bastards aboard?'

'What difference does it make, Bosun?' I asked. 'They could more easily come up the gangway at night.'

Which was true, but I had missed a significant point: baiting first-trippers was a traditional game with older seamen, particularly if they were cadets from whom such as bosuns would take orders some day. But for me such a day seemed unattainably remote.

For four years I had to resign myself to taking orders from

Dasher Daly and work alongside the crew. We hosed down the decks each morning; holystoned the timber decks of the bridge and boat-decks; replaced ropes in frayed rigging and blocks and tackle; and always there was rust to chip and consequent red-leading and painting to be done. The perpetual drumming of hammers striking metal was a shipboard noise that dominated all others, and even penetrated one's dreams. I can hear it yet.

When we stopped work for meals, I would peel off my denims, usually tacky from my inept painting technique, don my uniform and dine in the saloon, there to be waited on by stewards and to exchange relatively civilized conversation with the officers. The meal over, I was back into working togs and wielding paintbrush or marlinspike again to the accompaniment of chatter that wasn't at all civilized and often incomprehensible, though I guessed it was heavily seasoned with sexual innuendo. It was a sort of Jekyll-and-Hyde existence.

Yet despite the costume changes, the unaccustomed hard work and the blistering heat which soon took the skin off my back, I was deeply contented and happy to be a cadet in a deep-sea tramp sailing to romantic lands. I wouldn't have changed places with those former collegians who were sailing with big ships or coasters. Cadets on liners, it seemed to me, would lead highly artificial lives, always decorously dressed so as to be presentable to passengers with whom they were encouraged to be agreeable, sipping cocktails at the captain's exclusive parties, and dancing with millionairesses to the music of the ship's orchestra. No chipping rust for them or getting bawled out by surly bosuns; but they would not experience the reality of the salty tang of the elements or the workaday swing and rhythm of life aboard a tramp steamer. Storms would be a nuisance to a liner, but to a small vessel they were natural enemies with which men and ship grappled for survival.

And yet there were few more desolating occasions on board than seeing a liner at night with all its lights ablaze and the sometimes audible sounds of music and laughter drifting across the waves. As the big ship disappeared, there followed a desolating loneliness so intense that no one felt like talking for a while, and the night seemed blacker than before.

As for coasters, the crews had the advantage of frequent visits home, but the monotony of short trips to the Continent or round the home ports could become unbearably tedious. The popular distinction between the two types of merchant vessels ran thus: if the captain of a coaster loses sight of land, his bowels fail him; whereas if the master of a deep-sea boat sights land, he suffers the same distressing experience. At that time, our captain's digestive system was under no threat. What coastlines we saw were barely visible through the haze on the horizon. Sardinia, Tunisia and Sicily were passed at a steady ten knots in perfect weather, the sea to the south like a burnished shield. Only when Malta had been left behind and there was nothing but sea between us and our destination did the weather change, and that with fierce suddenness.

Storms in the Mediterranean can be swift, brief and drastic. They lunge at ships with demented fury as though they bear them a grudge. Heralded by grey skies and quickening seas, the equinoctial storm that struck the ship head on took us by surprise and the watch were sent scurrying into action, turning main ventilators from the wind, rigging lifelines, bowsing up deck cargo more securely. The look-out was taken off the fo'c'sle and installed in the comparative safety of monkey island. The sea leapt wildly and the wind keened like a mad thing until at the height of the storm a crescendo was reached and the ship bucked and lurched and heeled with every oncoming monstrous wave. In that kind of sea the distance between wave-crests is short so that sometimes the vessel protrudes unsupported from a wave before reaching the next, and she falls crashing into the trough with a sickening explosive *crack* and you'd swear the keelson has snapped. By then the new wave has thundered down on the decks in a tumultuous hissing deluge.

Even when the wind had dropped and the glass had risen, the waves were still running high, and the ship rose and fell like a scenic railway, shattering crockery in the pantry and cramping my stomach into knots. Yet I was exhilarated by it all, and relieved that I hadn't succumbed to seasickness. This must prove something, I thought.

On the third evening of the storm I decided that it was time I learnt some helmsmanship, so after dinner I went up to the wheelhouse with the third mate. There was no rain, but the low, heavy cloud had reduced visibility to a dangerous extent. Spiers, a young ordinary seaman, was at the wheel, which writhed and twisted under his grasp like a living thing, the light from the wobbling binnacle casting an eerie glow over his ruddy features. I was thinking of Gauguin's painting of Jacob wrestling with the angel when the Old Man and the second mate came in arguing about the exact location of Port Said. The second was in charge of navigation and he was getting the blame for the storm which had blown us off course. 'It should be about three points on the starboard bow, sir,' he said, 'by my calculations, making allowances for the gale.'

'Yes, Mr Travis,' said the captain testily. 'But it isn't. So where the bloody hell has the damn place got to? That's what I want to know! Come on, let's see from the bridge.' And he led the way out, the mates and myself following, in search of Port Said.

My eyesight was good and although the others had binoculars, it wasn't long before I had spotted a faint quiver of light to starboard as the ship reared above the surrounding waves. To be certain, I waited till the ship plunged, then rose again. I saw it a second time, hardly more than a flutter on the horizon, slightly paler in tone than the clouds. But it was a light, and it was spasmodic. It could not be a ship.

'Over there, sir!' I called out, pointing in its direction.

The captain swivelled round and seemed to notice me for the first time. 'You mean the light, boyo? Where d'you see it?'

I pointed towards the light again.

The third mate confirmed its position, and orders were given to Spiers. The ship lumberingly veered round and the seas struck us beam on, throwing men from their bunks and renewing havoc in the kitchen and pantry. But we were on course.

I felt like a true seaman, and tomorrow I should set foot in Egypt.

5

First Landfall

I awoke just before first light, missing the beat of the engines and, dressing hurriedly, went out on deck. The pilot was clambering up the Jacob's ladder, the mate waiting to greet him. The storm had blown itself out, or we had sailed away from its direction, and there was only a slight swell to mark its passing. The waves had a bloom of pale jade about them, a reflection of the delicate green sky with its fringe of saffron deepening to rose on the horizon. The land was flatter than any coast I had seen before, merely a dark line stretching on either side of the port which, as the light strengthened, began to appear as a jumble of squarish buildings, dusky white, with the occasional dome and minaret silhouetted against the sky. An offshore breeze brought a mingled waft of odours, a strange combination of baked sand, decaying fruit, dry sanitation and unknown herbs: an arid, spicy, unforgettable smell.

As the engines chuntered into life and the ship got underway, the sun broke clear above Sinai, revealing a cluster of shipping in the harbour, docking for coal like our own vessel or waiting to go through the canal. There were splendid liners with white hulls and gold funnels; P&O boats bound for India, Union Castle ships heading for South Africa; and an assortment of freighters and cargo passengers. And moored among the steamships and motor-turbine luxury vessels were Arab sailing craft, sturdy dhows and graceful lateen-rigged feluccas, some of which, tied to rusty mooring buoys, dipped gently in the swell like sleeping gulls.

We drew nearer the port, and the high articulated wail of a muezzin drifted over the waters from an unseen minaret. Arabs emerged on decks, knelt on rush mats and prayed to Mecca with fervency and a total lack of self-consciousness.

To starboard, the buildings gained clarity, blue-domed port authority offices, the emporium of Simon Artz, the shops bright with Eastern merchandise; and before these, the green statue of de Lesseps waved a theatrical arm towards the Orient.

The *Rembrandt* was bound for a humbler destination, and an hour later the ship was moored alongside a coaling berth. By then the bum-boats had found us and the decks seethed with vendors, grinning and chattering and laden with goods: tooled leather handbags, ornamental cushion covers, fly-whisks, fruits of every description, pornographic photographs which made my jaw drop. And something called Spanish fly.

But no one had time for explanations, for the crew were kept busy battening down, locking everything that could be locked, and making fast all ports, for the coal-wallahs would soon be at work and their thieving was legendary.

The method of loading coal could not have been more primitive. Two long gangplanks were lashed in place between the quay and the deck at number three hatch, the 'tween deck hold of which was to be used for coal storage. This was filled by a chain of almost naked Arabs, each carrying a sack of about half a hundredweight. They trotted up one plank, emptied their sacks and returned down the adjacent plank. Once ashore the empty sacks were exchanged for full ones with hardly a pause, and the human chain continued this circular action throughout the long day. More slowly, so did the sun, and long before noon the sweating, dusky bodies were caked with coal-dust. And as they kept up the jogging rhythm they intoned a work-chant to lighten their labours: *ay-wa . . . ay-wa . . . ay-wa!*

So this was a remnant of the civilization which was the fountainhead for all the others. Yet the word was the Arabic expression for the affirmative. Despite their lot, they said *yes* to life. They were at the bottom of the heap but were not defeated. Allah was merciful. *Ay-wa! . . .*

After lunch and pay-up time, I was glad to escape ashore and away from the din, the monotonous chanting, the grime and dust that filled the air and penetrated everything.

'Hullo there!' a voice called out, just as I had stepped into the ferry-boat. It was Bill the donkeyman. He clambered aboard and settled on the after-thwart. The boatman pushed off and rowed standing up, facing the direction of travel.

'You haven't been to these parts before, I reckon,' Bill said when I referred to this odd means of propulsion. He knew I hadn't, and when he suggested we should team up for the afternoon, I got the impression he was really offering his services as a chaperone. Minto and the other junior officers had stayed on board to guard their belongings, so I decided to accept Bill's offer.

As soon as we stepped ashore on the town side, I was glad of this, for we were immediately surrounded by a horde of Arab kids brandishing trinkets and gewgaws, and hawking wares and touting custom for an astonishing variety of services.

'You want shoe-clean, Johnee ... I give!' We were wearing sandals.

'Newspepper, Johnee, you buy?' They were a fortnight old.

'You like naughtee pictures. I got ...'

'Hey, effendi! You want Spanish fly? I got. Good for *zhubric*!'

'What's Spanish fly, Bill?'

'Tell you later, Jock. ... Go on, scarper, you lot! *Imshi!*'

'Johnee, you like my seester, yes? Very good for you. Very clean. She schoolteacher. ...'

I was horror-struck: that a kid of six or seven could procure for his sister, whether she was a well-scrubbed pillar of the educational establishment or not, sickened me to the roots of my Presbyterian conscience. I had older sisters of my own.

Bill must have realized something of what I felt, for his protests grew more vehement: 'Go on, bugger off, the lot of you. ... *Y'ala!*'

But it was hopeless, and they gathered round like the black flies which were everywhere. Finally the donkeyman, using his bulk, lunged through their midst, forcibly driving them apart. They quickly trailed after him, some clutching his tropical jacket, and I was reminded of an illustration I had seen of Gulliver towing the Lilliputian fleet. I hurried into his wake.

'Hey, meester! You big Pasha, yes?'

The kids laughed at this sally, and I guessed that their importunities were a sport for them, a means of reducing the dignity of the white man, who was not only an infidel but whose style of life was an affront to their poverty and deprivation. The profit motive may have been a secondary consideration.

Bill knew his way around and, making sure I was following, he dodged into a narrow street where gangs of marauding kids would not be tolerated by the merchants and tradesmen whose shops lined either side. In between the displays of carpets and silks, coppersmiths and leather workers plied their crafts in open doorways. There was a delicious odour of baked bread, and weird formless Arabic music issued from several unshuttered windows. At little cafés groups of seated Arabs dressed in *jallabahs* sucked at tubes leading from glass bottles in which a watery liquid fumed and seethed.

'Hubbly-bubbly,' said Bill, adding by way of explanation the single word 'hashish'.

Both terms meant nothing to me, but looking at the dull, vacant expressions of the squatting Arabs, I supposed they were smoking some kind of drug. They neither conversed nor smiled, nor even acknowledged each other's existence; so whatever esoteric joys were being experienced, the effects were kept secret, confined within the turbaned heads of the smokers. As a social activity, it seemed to be the loneliest in the world.

I was thankful to emerge from the street and into the light and bustle of a huge square, the bazaar, where dozens of stalls were set up around a central area in which symmetrical rows of melons were piled. Some stately bedouins rode in on magnificent horses, making for the camel market beyond the stalls where seated dromedaries lifted their heads and groaned horribly, showing dangerous-looking teeth. Merchants wandered by with laden asses and mules, stopping to finger items of textiles on display. The air buzzed with flies and the sounds of half a dozen languages.

We found a restaurant catering for Europeans under a colonnade with a view of the bazaar, and sipped cooling drinks flavoured with mint. Sometimes a street-vendor would approach, if the owner were indoors, and repeat the offers of merchandise with which I had by now become familiar, in name if not description.

'Get out, you bloody fellahin!' shouted Bill at one party of Arab kids.

'*Imshi*,' I called after them. 'In fact, *Imshi y'ala!*' I was picking up the lingo fast enough but there were other things I wanted to learn. 'You were going to tell me what Spanish fly is. . . .'

Bill was instantly evasive, his manner resembling that of my older relatives when awkward subjects were raised. They would purse their lips, look uncomfortable and reply with half-truths. Bill did all of these.

'Don't bother buying any, Jock. It's likely to be fake anyway.'

'But fake what?'

'Well . . . it's supposed to be an aphrodisiac.'

'What's that?'

Bill sighed and mopped his brow, then abandoning prevarication he blurted out: 'It's a love potion, like. An inducement to sexual stimulation. After Aphrodite, Goddess of Love, and all that.'

'I see! . . . In that case I've no need for the stuff.'

This was true, for recently, I had become aware that my problem was quite the reverse, and I stared moodily at the robed girls who passed and wondered if the faces behind their yashmaks were as lovely as the lustrous eyes that gazed demurely ahead. Then I remembered my father's depressing warnings about Eastern women, and the immediate future looked bleak. The market scene before me was as colourfully exotic as anything I had imagined about the East, but the chances of meeting a legitimate schoolteacher were remote.

'Hey, effendi!' An Arab youth with rheumy eyes popped his head over our table. 'You like exhibeetions? I take you. . . .'

This sounded better, and my spirits rose, for I hadn't seen any paintings worthy of the name since the Royal Scottish Academy's summer show. Art had been one of my best subjects at school. Moreover, there were bound to be a few female art students there, copying the Masters, comparing techniques.

'What about it, Bill? I'd like to know a little about Egyptian art.'

'Jock . . . it's not that kind of exhibition.'

Bill seemed uncomfortable again, and I suspected that he wished he had left me at the quayside.

'What kind of exhibition is it, then?'

'You like, Johnee. Very good. Very naughtee,' said the kid, who had been listening to our remarks with a puzzled expression, as though to say: What other kinds of exhibition are there?

The restaurant owner came out and chased the little Arab with a barage of abuse beyond the range of our vocabulary. When peace was restored, Bill addressed himself to my question and, with plenty of circumlocution, he described in broad outline a few of the sexual entertainments available to tourists in Port Said, diversions as disgusting as they were improbable. I felt sick again, not only at the degradation of the human spirit that such acts entailed, but at the hideous cynicism with which the organizers of these 'exhibitions' included tiny children in the performances.

'But who's to blame, Jock?' said the donkeyman. 'The poverty-stricken Arabs? Or the pampered Westerner out for new sensations? Without their money, there'd be no exhibitions.'

I couldn't answer him, for I was trying hard not to think of gigantic mulattos and infants no older than my niece; and versatile girls and trained donkeys . . .

'Another thing,' said Bill. 'Without the canal, there'd be no Port Said. So you could say it's as much de Lesseps' fault as anyone's for bringing all those tourists here with time on their hands and money to burn. It takes two sorts of people to produce decadence. The wealthy and the needy. Thank your stars you belong to neither group, Jock. We musn't be smug, must we?'

After all the intervening years I can hardly vouch for the accuracy of my memory to that extent: those may not have been Bill's exact words, but that is the gist of them and they left a deep impression. There was compassion and understanding in his remarks, and a veiled reproof against priggishness which showed he had recognized this feature of my character. Only later did I appreciate that no one else on board could have revealed this fault with more tact, or given a less libidinous account of the vices of Port Said, which is why, I think, he had chosen to give it.

He followed his homily with a breezy laugh as though apologizing for being too serious, then with a sharp alteration of manner, he suddenly whispered: 'Look out! It's the gulli-gulli man. Keep your hands in your pockets!'

Coming towards us under the colonnade was a tall Arab wearing the usual fez but swathed in dark voluminous robes. As relentless as fate, he came to a halt at our table quite deaf to Bill's rudimentary Arabic. The few dismissive words had now become reflex actions, like the swatting of flies. 'Gulli-gulli-gulli,' he murmured with all the solemnity of a sacred incantation, and proceeded to pluck objects, most of them living, from our pockets and ears with immense skill. Soon the table was littered with his materializations, and tiny chickens peep-peeped and scuttered around the glasses and saucers in bewildering confusion. Two white doves fluttered down from nowhere.

The success of his virtuosity seemed to depend not only on the seductive sound of his incantation but on the regular exchange of piastres. Sensing that the flow of coins was drying up, he waved incredibly flexible hands over his equipment and livestock, and they vanished into the complicated folds of his *jallabah* as mysteriously as they had come. He paused from his intoning to announce that for a mere ten piastres he would perform the most amazing trick of all – he himself would disappear! By that time we were almost hypnotized by the man, and if he had faded into a column of smoke before our eyes it would have been no more than we expected.

'Gulli-gulli-gulli,' he resumed after swallowing the coins; then, slowly raising his golden eyes to the heavens so that in our entranced state we were obliged to do likewise, he swiftly turned on his heel and, with laden robes swaying, glided down the colonnade and moved smartly round a corner and out of sight.

In all, the ship pulled into Port Said five times, but I never saw the gulli-gulli man again, so perhaps he really did vanish. Under the effects of Western culture the street entertainers would find it hard to earn a living, and the gulli-gulli man's magic would be overwhelmed by the greater wonders of radio, cinema and, eventually, television.

A troupe of acrobats was next on the scene, and after they had run through their act and tumbled off to more lucrative restaurants, an old man playing bagpipes followed by a boy with a tabor strolled past. Nothing could have distilled the essence of the East more than that weird melody which, without beginning or end, or musical phrasing detectable to our ears, looped and twirled and shook out its intricate coils above the undifferentiated beat of the boy's drum. A haunting, evocative, almost elegiac sound that trembled in the mind long after the musicians had padded softly away into distance.

The sun was falling: after a dish of *cous-cous*, unleavened cakes and Turkish coffee, we left the restaurant and made our way back to the ship, which was due to leave port that evening.

The harbour waters were now tranquil with a milky sheen reflecting a sky of opal, and the hulls and masts of ships. A few stars emerged more brilliant than any I had seen at home, even in the Highlands. With an almost audible *plop* the sun did a nosedive into the western sea, and soon the muezzins were calling from the minarets and Arabs were dropping to their knees, in the streets, on the wharfs, and on the decks of the sailing craft. Allah was merciful, for toil was over for another day. Praise be to Allah.

The coal-wallahs had finished their work and the gangplanks had been removed from amidships. The ship was black and filthy with a coating of coal-dust, but all was quiet and peaceful. I had a leisurely shower, then dressed and went into the saloon for dinner.

'How was Port Said?' asked Minto.

I thought about the colourful exoticism of the bazaar, the pestilential street-vendors, the emblematic beauty of the bagpipe's song, the gulli-gulli man. And the 'exhibitions'.

'It's like a rainbow shining over a cesspit,' I said. Then I remembered something. 'How were the coal-wallahs? Did they steal anything?'

'Ah,' said Minto, with an embarrassed shrug. 'Only your civvy raincoat.'

'Only!' I cried.

'Well, you've still got your uniform coat. And it won't rain for ages. I had to leave the cabin for a moment, you see. Sorry.'

So was I. It had been almost new, a Christmas present from my mother.

The fourth engineer piped up: 'Anyway, Jock, we bought you a melon to console you for your great loss. It was delicious.'

'Thank you. That was very considerate,' I said. 'But I didn't see a melon in the cabin. You ate it all?'

'Ah, Jock,' said Minto again, which seemed to be his way of introducing bad news. 'I'm afraid the cockroaches got into your half. So I had to heave it over the wall.'

At that moment I felt like heaving Minto over the side after the melon; but later I realized that if I had stayed aboard to safeguard my gear like the others, I should have missed the experience of Port Said; its contrasts and variety, the squalor and the splendour. On the way back, I had mounted a camel – a difficult process – to be photographed by an Egyptian with a mouthful of gold teeth who claimed to know my father. On subsequent trips if I passed that way, I would be greeted with a glittering smile and a cheerful yell: 'Meester Green! I knew your fadder, he engineer, yes?' Possibly he may not have known his own.

I can't recall how he learnt of my name, but meeting the son of an acquaintance seemed to give him great pleasure, and I felt rather less of a stranger because of it in that exotic town. A raincoat was a small price to pay. All day the Arabs had clamoured for baksheesh. They had finally got it.

It was dark when we set sail for Haifa except for a girdle of rosy light around the horizon and the brilliance of stars that studded the blue dome of the sky.

6

Palestine

None of the crew was sorry to see Palestine slip astern and vanish into darkness; not just because of the sporadic three-cornered fighting that was going on – there was a similar state of undercover hostilities awaiting us in Greece, yet we felt genuine regret when we left that country. But in Palestine we were made aware of a tangled skein of opposing interests that did not seem capable of resolution. A country of intermingled Muslims, Jews and minor Christian sects, all more or less of the same genetic race, and most of them shepherds, farm workers and fishermen, were suddenly invaded by huge numbers of urbanized European Jews. The new mixture was bound to be explosive. Previously the principal groups had achieved an equilibrium, a working arrangement. The influx had created a dangerous imbalance, and British troops had been moved in to instil order and to permit the transition of the country to proceed. It was an impossible task, for no attempt was made to treat the various factions as equals. An army captain I met, who was in charge of some civil works near Haifa, explained that on pay-days the labourers were lined up in two ranks because the rates were differentiated between the incomers and the Palestinians, whether Hebrew or not, greatly to the advantage of immigrants.

'And who has taken these decisions, gentlemen?' asked the chief engineer at tiffin one sultry afternoon, and then answered his own question: 'Our old friends the statesmen, at their favourite game of carving up the world, realigning boundaries, eliminating some states and creating others in their place.'

'I believe the original decision to define the State of Israel was taken after the First World War,' said the chief sparks. 'So we're witnessing historic events.'

The chief engineer gave a snort of disgust: 'Then they ought to have spent the interim examining the issues. What we're witnessing, in fact, are the death-throes of Palestine and the birth-pangs of Israel simultaneously. Truly brilliant. Even a Port Said coal-wallah could have predicted disaster. I wish some of those parliamentary sods could witness the havoc they cause.'

'You can't make an omelette without breaking eggs,' murmured Mr Gregan, but before the chief could turn on him there was the sound of an almighty explosion and we hurried out on deck.

A tanker had blown up and a towering column of flame and smoke was leaping into the sky.

'That was no accident,' said the chief. 'Saboteurs, probably.'

We watched the fire-fighting launches race across the harbour and douse the flames with their powerful hoses, and wondered if any of the crew had survived. Later that evening the saloon wireless set was tuned in to the local radio station. There was no mention of the incident and the communiqué concluded with the daily list of British servicemen casualties.

By day the streets of Haifa were quiet enough except for the rumble of trolley-cars, but at night the rattle of gunfire in the suburbs was not uncommon. While Jew and Arab fought each other in this back-street clandestine fashion, both parties gunned down stray British servicemen who got in the way. The troops were armed at all times, therefore, even off duty, and this led to an episode that nearly transported me to a more peaceful world. The third mate and I had discovered a small café some way from the centre of town, run by a charming French woman of about thirty and her young assistant of indeterminate nationality. The café was not elegant or distinguished for its cuisine, but we had become weary of the cabarets with the endless singsongs of drunken soldiery, and Madame Jeanne discouraged the patronage of other ranks. This was what attracted us to the café. On our second visit it was clear that Madame Jeanne was attracted to the third mate, and the price of our John Collins underwent a sharp reduction, a drink to which I was partial since it consisted mainly of fruit salad. The omelettes began to improve and the platefuls of petit fours were heaped to capacity. The third mate was not long in showing his appreciation of these improvements to the service, and it became standard practice for Madame to close the louvered shutters to the windows and lock the doors while they went upstairs for half an hour or so.

I was left with ample *petit fours*, a full glass, and the company of the assistant whose name was Selima, a girl of about my own age. Her English was scant, and since my few Arabic terms were mainly abusive, conversation between us soon limped to a standstill. Madame had made sure there were no customers during these interruptions to the working day, and when we were left alone like this I was conscious of an indefinably charged quality in the atmosphere, something almost electric and oppressive. Nothing like this had happened at school or college dances, and I was at a loss to know how to act. She must have been aware of it too, for under the pale olive complexion her Levantine features were strained and disturbed. Then one night the storm burst. She had refused my third offer of biscuits, and I had drunk as many John Collins, when she grabbed my arms and pulled me into the back premises where she had a small room off the kitchen, from which it borrowed light.

We both knew that Madame and the third would be down soon, and I guessed that her employer would not be pleased to find us thus occupied. This lent urgency to what in any case was a pretty frantic business, a matter of grappling with suddenly recalcitrant clothing, of inaccurate fumbling and probing until the hot, viscous connection was made. The warnings of my father faded to a distant murmur on the horizon of my mind, and unaccountably an inapt quotation floated to the surface of it: 'Don't shoot till you see the whites of their eyes!' That was about all I could see of the girl as we rocked and panted on the narrow bed; until a piercing white light enveloped the universe, and some fundamental part of me took wing into an infinite region from which consciousness itself was excluded.

A thunderous knocking at the café doors brought me back to earth. We struggled into our clothes and reached the café just as Madame and the third were coming downstairs. I think they guessed what we had been up to, but Madame Jeanne did not pause and went straight to the doors, where she looked through the slats at the visitor. There was no glass in the doors or windows. 'Go away!' she cried out. 'Only officers here! Not for you.'

I teetered back to my table and sat down. For the first time in my life I needed a drink that would not merely quench thirst. Gradually I began to take in impressions from the outside world. I hardly dared look at Selima, who was standing behind the beaded curtain that separated the café from the kitchen.

It seemed our visitor had not been dissuaded, and moments later I found myself looking through the slats at an unsteady British soldier levelling an equally unsteady revolver at my head. 'Better let me in, mate,' he said. 'Or you get this.' He sounded drunk, so whether he was bluffing or not made no difference, since he might shoot anyway. I don't remember being afraid, but this may have had something to do with the recent stupendous event in Selima's room. All the same, I was determined not to show fear, and in this I was helped by the third who had joined me and who kept his head; and Madame Jeanne who simply repeated her advice to the man to go away: '*Allez! Fil d'un cochon*. . . . I get the *gendarmes militaires*!' she shouted as an afterthought, adding a few choice words of French in which *merde* and *canaille* were distinguishable.

But she had miscalculated, and the next instant he had blazed away, firing several rounds through the shutters, one of which nearly parted my hair on the wrong side. We dropped below the table, Madame finally crawling on all fours to the light-switch by the door. We felt easier when the place was plunged in darkness, and we raised our heads above the sill to see how matters stood with the persistent caller. He was still wavering around, pointing his pistol this way and that, not sure where to fire next.

Madame Jeanne's next move puzzled me, but I shouldn't have been surprised: she wanted to prevent the third's head from being blown off. She opened the doors and let the man in, hastily drawing the bolt after him. The soldier was led through the kitchen and presumably out of the back door. Possibly Madame gave him a drink, for some minutes elapsed before she returned. In retrospect, it may be that he, too, had experienced improved omelettes and a profusion of *petit fours* in his time. It's always difficult for a lover on the way out.

Shortly after the man's departure a Jeep pulled up outside, replete with armed military police, and once more the doors resounded with clamorous visitors.

'Madame Jeanne! Open up, we know he's in there!' called out

a sergeant, which made the third and me suspect we had intruded into a local drama that had been continuing for some time. Meanwhile our roles had been merely walk-on parts, of no real significance to the outcome. This was probably everyday stuff in Haifa. We decided to let them get on with it, and leave.

Madame Jeanne took a similar view; but first she hurled invective at the military police, then she took the third's sleeve and whispered fervently that he must not abandon her, and that she would be desolate if he did not return tomorrow.

'Come along, lady!' said the sergeant. 'We ain't got all night.'

Then he opened the flap of his holster and once again I was staring at the cylindrical end of a revolver. The room was still in darkness but the lights from the streets cast a faint reflection, and the godlike calm induced by my making love with Selima had deserted me. This was no longer happening to some sublunary, unimportant part of me. A bullet could be painful. Or fatal.

'Your last warning, Madame, before we fire,' said the sergeant.

'A demain, mon cher!' said Madame Jeanne, kissing the third with a juicy smack. She shook my hand and with dispatch escorted us out through the back door before I had time to see Selima again and explain that we wouldn't be back tomorrow, or the next day, or the next month or even perhaps at all. . . . For that was the way of things. We were seamen, and the ship was bound for Tel Aviv at dawn, and from there to Greece, and only by the remotest chance would we sail back to Haifa again.

7

Man Overboard

In Tel Aviv there was a stevedore who went one better than the gulli-gulli man. We were anchored off in a running sea, unloading into a string of lighters. I was on cargo-watch. A brisk offshore wind whittled the wave-crests which moved across the bay in livid corrugations, causing the lighters to buck and rear like tethered wild horses, scattering brilliant sunlit foam. Some of the cargo was scheduled for United Nations relief centres, from which it would be distributed to refugee camps; but there was more alcoholic drink in the consignment than foodstuffs, which led the ironically minded to ponder afresh on the term 'displaced persons', as refugees were then known. There was also a fair amount of personal baggage in the 'tween deck of number four hold which unwise colonials had shipped over-seas, and which was particularly alluring to thieves. Catching them was the difficulty. As I stood at the hatch coaming watching the Arabs wrestling with bales and crates, fitting them on slings or cargo trays, I knew it was going on literally under my nose. But they were too quick for me: I could never prove which among that gang of fellahin were the culprits. They looked and dressed alike, perhaps deliberately so, to escape detection, and I did not feel enthusiastic about frisking the burnous or *jallabah* of a native in the darkness of the hold.

Then I saw him. A sudden gust of wind had heeled the ship just enough to allow a shaft of sunlight to penetrate a corner of the 'tween deck. An Arab was busily stuffing the contents of a slashed suitcase into his robe. Acting on impulse, I scrambled over the coaming and down the ladder as quickly as I could; but in that instant my back was turned, he climbed up some crates across the hold from me and was hoisting himself to the deck. By the time I had ascended again he was gone. The decks were empty except for the winchmen. He had to be in one of the lighters; so once more I didn't stop to think but threw a leg over the deck-rail and jumped down to the crazily dancing bows of the nearest lighter. So began a weird chase. There were six lighters strung out in a line, all of them rocking madly in the swell, a shifting kaleidoscope of light and shadow. I hunted through one lighter, making sure it contained no lurking thief, then hauled on the hawser of the next one till its bows were under my stern, then let go and leapt. The man knew what was happening, for sometimes I glimpsed the hood of a burnous as he too crossed from one barge to another. I tried to improve my barge-hopping, but when I reached the last lighter of all, there was still no trace of him. He had vanished with his plunder as though by means of oriental magic, and for a while I stood there as the glittering town of Tel Aviv with its white domes and minarets rose and fell, and I found myself muttering, gulli-gulli-gulli. . . .

When I had time to think about it, I was glad he had disappeared, for what chance would I have had against a desperate native, armed, likely enough, with one of those curved daggers I had seen in the bazaars of Port Said? Even if any of the crew had seen my foolhardy pursuit of the man, assistance would have come too late and I would have been food for the fish. I thought of Newport and deplored my impulsiveness. The chase had been exhilarating – a hunt usually is: but the hunter might have become the quarry, and I resolved not to act the amateur policeman again. The cargo was well insured, I had learnt. So be it.

The next day Tel Aviv had vanished too, and our course was set for Volos on the east coast of Greece. Winter was approaching and we should have been sailing to meet it, but as we passed Rhodes and entered the Dodecanese the atmosphere became freakishly warm under a blanket of cloud. And it was there that I had my first taste of *déjà vu*. It was more: not only did I have an irrational conviction that I had sailed that way before, but I felt an uncanny sense of returning home. Maybe the islands had evoked recollections of myths and legends I had absorbed as a child, of Jason and Ulysses and Theseus. Or perhaps I had inherited genes from a forbear, a classical scholar, who may have returned home via Greece from Russia where he had been tutor to a grand duke. Then there is the time theory of J.W. Dunne which suggests that the future already exists and that only our faulty memory system prevents our seeing what lies ahead. But the most fanciful and most appealing notion of all derives from a national belief that the Scots were descendants of Scythian tribes who migrated westwards from the Black Sea area. They would certainly have lingered in the benign climate of Greece until forced out by more powerful invasions: in which case, possibly I had experienced an echo of racial memory, a sensation of familiarity and kinship as strong as it was mysterious, and which faded from my mind only when the ship reached mainland waters and entered the Trikeri Straits. A curious name, and one that applied in its Anglicized form most aptly to the condition of Greece at the time.

The first hint that something was amiss appeared when the pilot, who had taken us through the Gulf of Pagasai and into the bay of Volos, insisted on being paid in kind; in this case, a couple of pounds of white sugar. Once ashore we found out why: the retreating German army of occupation had swamped the banking system with fake money and the country was in financial chaos. They had left other, more sinister legacies, but those came to light only later, to the chagrin of the beneficiaries.

We dropped anchor about two cable lengths from the town, and the pilot, with his peculiar fee, was put aboard the launch at nightfall. In the morning we found ourselves in a fiordlike natural harbour bounded by long, bare hills coated with frost. The sea, like the port of Volos, looked grey and inhospitable. No dolphins sported in the bay and no classical ruins adorned the town. Even the flotilla of cargo lighters that came bobbing towards us seemed dowdy and furtive as though anxious to avoid trouble: like the townsfolk themselves, as we discovered.

The war had dealt harshly with the Greeks, and the word *verboten* was frequently used. Yet they were not entirely cowed, for a strange little war was in progress, this one started by the British; and what was left of the Resistance movement was engaged in a series of skirmishes and a campaign of guerrilla action against their former allies.

Troops were stationed in the town, and a few of them visited the ship, partly for trading reasons but also to relieve the monotony of their cheerless lives. They were a most dispirited group of men. The good fight against fascism had been won; it was time to beat the swords into ploughshares, the tanks into tractors. But because of inscrutable higher politics they were forced to remain there and attempt to suppress Greek insurgents who had the bravest record of Nazi resistance in Europe. The few soldiers I met who understood the purpose of the war did not sympathize with it, and the rest simply wanted to go home, feeling it was none of their business.

The cause of the affair was explained to be my Stavros, a student employed as a tally clerk. 'Churchill good man for you,' he would say, then jerk his chin up, a Greek gesture for the negative, meaning 'not for Greece'.

Apparently the British war leader wanted to re-establish George of the Hellenes on the Greek throne on the dubious grounds that a related bunch of crowned heads would somehow ensure the stability of Europe, or at least unite a fair proportion of it against a potential enemy. But that hadn't worked in the past. According to Stavros, the Greeks did not want George back because he had deserted them when the Germans invaded the country; and besides, he was not a true son of Hellas, being of mixed Norwegian and German blood. And finally, the greatest gift which Greece had conferred on the world was the concept of democracy. Was it likely, I was asked, that the people would take kindly to a foreign monarch thrust upon them for political reasons without popular consent?

I knew that the guerrillas were communists for the most part, but I was ignorant of international statecraft, and I had no answers to give. In those days communism was not openly considered to be a threat to world peace. It was too soon after Stalin's victories on the Eastern front, and the cumbersome process of turning the propaganda machinery in the opposite direction had not yet begun. In the minds of many, Russia was still our glorious ally: Stavros suggested that since the war, Russia was Greece's only ally. British troops had fired on Resistance fighters in the Acropolis, did I know that? I didn't, and was horrified by the news. Even then the place was sacred to me.

But there were more immediate problems to contend with in Volos. As a means of delaying the Allied advance in Greece the

Germans had clinically injected unmarried young women with gonorrhoea, and the disease was rife in that part of the country. Its effects were quick to appear among some of the crew, and they were sent off to the army hospital for penicillin treatment. The local population was impoverished, and prostitution was more or less enforced on girls by needy parents, girls as ignorant of the disease as the young soldiers and seamen who made use of them. It was a commonplace story to those familiar with the ravages of war, but one not easily assimilated by a sixteen-year-old, and my education limped painfully forward.

It was assumed that, in order to afford these risky pleasures, the crew were plundering the cargo for bartering purposes, since no monies were issued to them, owing to the erratic exchange rates. Clothing and canned food were more valuable than the luckless drachma. It was winter and large overcoats, especially duffel-coats, could conceal quantities of both types of illegal tender. The crew members most efficient at this enterprise were Brownlee and Griffiths, two stokers who had signed on at Newport to replace my nocturnal assailants. In terms of comparative delinquency it was not much of a bargain, but the newcomers were cheerful Welshmen whose love of a tavern brawl was surpassed only by an irrepressible urge to sing wherever they found themselves, and often they would combine both activities with a happy disregard for the consequences.

It was my turn to be night-watchman again, but there was a variation to the routine at Volos. A Greek ferryman plied a whaler between the port and the ship during daylight hours, and after sunset the task fell to me. I would make about three trips ashore in the early evening, then around midnight loud hails from the quayside would rouse me from my book in the galley, and I would row across the dark harbour towards the lights of the tavernas on the sea-front, and then return the men to the ship. It was arduous work. On the way over their coats would be bulky with stolen goods, while on the reverse trips the men would be helplessly drunk and reeking of ouzo and resinated wine. Brownlee and Griffiths were regular passengers, and when they had concluded their business and enjoyments for the night, instead of bawling across the harbour for my services like the others, they were apt to lift their lusty voices in song. A particular favourite was 'None Shall Sleep' from Turandot, and coming from Brownlee and Griffiths in the small hours of the morning, it was no idle threat.

I never kept an account of who were still due to return, since some men stayed ashore and hitched a lift on the stevedores' boats at dawn. One night I must have assumed this to be the plan of the singing Welshmen, for I had missed the sound of melodious arias at the usual hour and, after two or three strenuous trips well after midnight, I was exhausted and fell asleep on the galley table. The next day I wished I hadn't. This is what happened, an account pieced together by various of the crew, including the modified version maintained by the Welshmen themselves.

After I had dozed off, the stokers, their cognac-enriched voices in good fettle, had arrived at the quayside and given the town a selection from their extensive repertoire. Sensing a prolonged delay, and not being men easily diverted from a desired goal, they knocked on every door of the waterfront houses until they had located a fisherman who agreed to ferry them to the ship. No doubt the bribes they offered were extravagant, but the night was cold, and there must have been something about the robust, devil-may-care attitude of his fares which aroused suspicion. This took the form of a persistent grumbling that continued after the boat was eased down the slipway and they had cast off. When they were half-way over, it began to affect the jovial spirits of the companions. They didn't like that.

'What's up with you, Dai,' asked Brownlee. 'Aren't you happy at your work?' A common inquiry among seamen.

At that, the fisherman shipped oars and explained as best he could that he would row no further until he had been paid, if not in money then in kind, and he fingered the cloth of their duffel-coats.

The friends replied patiently that their money was on board and that they had no intention of parting with such useful apparel.

The fisherman repeated his ultimatum, his voice taking on a querulous note, and he made as though to turn the boat around.

'Shall we pay him, Griffiths bach?'

'Nobody ever said we don't settle our accounts,' said the other, and jointly they grabbed the man and heaved him over the side. Quickly they took up the oars and were soon skimming towards the gangway. Once they were on board, the boat was allowed to drift away; and the two friends who were quite convinced, as they remarked later, that 'those Greek boyos float like corks', went aft to their quarters to sleep like children with not a care in the world.

The donkeyman wakened me a few minutes before the second cook and the galley-boy came in to make breakfast. A close thing, for they were insatiable gossips and would have spread the word around that I had been asleep on watch. In the mariner's scale of ethics, I surmised this to be a cardinal crime.

The dimarchos arrived with the chief of police shortly after breakfast. The mate had seen the police launch swerve gracefully up to the gangway and the civic officials, with rather less grace, mount purposefully to the deck. Formal courtesies were exchanged, then, at their request, the mate guided them up the companionway to the captain's suite.

It must have been a difficult interview, for the sound of the Old Man's outraged bellows carried all the way to the stewards' pantry, where tasks causing the least noise were suddenly adopted. A townsman had been almost drowned by two members of the crew, they heard. 'Big men liking to sing much.' A fair description of Brownlee and Griffiths, they thought, as they polished tumblers and made sandwiches. The man had managed to swim ashore and he alerted the astinomia when he recovered from his ordeal. But the captain had protested the innocence of his crew in the matter and demanded that the civic dignitaries produce witnesses. The dimarchos retorted with a counter-proposal that an identification parade should be arranged, there and then, since their unfortunate townsman was waiting in the launch for this very purpose.

After that, the voices were curiously muted, and it was speculated that the Old Man had backed down and was negotiating terms. This, the officials seemed ready to do; and they may have anticipated it from the outset, for they had brought no armed police with them. Just as well for the police, thought the stewards, for it would have been a brave party who attempted to tackle Brownlee and Griffiths in a small launch.

It was fully an hour before the supposition was confirmed. The chief steward was summoned to a room filled with the aroma of good cigars and malt whisky, and ordered to procure certain quantities of foodstuffs from the stores. These were parcelled up and lowered into the launch, the crew of two reaching up to receive them. For the first time we noticed a forlorn figure sitting in the stern-sheets staring dully around him while he waited for the enactment of justice.

It occurred to us that the acquisition of a few pounds of sugar and flour from the supplies of the malefactors was a more practical form of retribution than the imprisonment of the culprits in that straitened community. Justice was an abstraction but the people were hungry. If Brownlee and Griffiths had been arrested, there would have been two more mouths to feed.

As for the singing Welshmen, the launch was hardly underway when they were ordered to appear before the Old Man. A steward found it necessary to polish some brasswork in the captain's alleyway. His report went as follows:

'Well, now . . . I suppose it was you two who were responsible for last night's escapade?'

'What escapade was that, Captain?'

'You know damn well what I'm talking about! The mayor was here, and the chief of police, and they made no mistake about you. It cost the company a pretty penny to get rid of them, I can tell you. And it's coming off your wages!'

'But Captain, sir, we aren't getting any wages!'

'Don't interrupt. Do you realize you almost killed a man?'

There was a pause, and the steward visualized the stokers chewing the ends of their sweat-rags as they deduced that the fisherman had survived his immersion. 'I told you those boyos float like corks, Griffiths,' Brownlee was heard to murmur.

This provoked a yell of rage and a torrent of invective from the captain, as he described their characters, ancestries and probable fates in colourful detail, and which only an exhausted vocabulary or the sound of the lunch-gong forced him to discontinue. The stokers were dismissed, and they capered from the room, a look of simulated contrition on their black faces.

'Mind what I said, you bloody Welshmen, you!' roared the captain, his head round the door. 'Or I'll make damn sure you'll never sail again this side of hell!'

It was a convincing performance, but as Griffiths passed the steward, he winked and opened his shirt to reveal a bottle of rum. The Old Man had felt remorse at the ferocious dressing-down he had given his fellow countrymen and had made suitable amends.

He was like that: blustering and authoritarian to the crew yet quick to defend them against whatever landsmen might threaten them with. He reserved the right to take punitive measures on his men, but he was fiercely protective towards them when local police or port authorities tried to do the same. Captain Davis was a paternalist. He believed that seamen were innately different from other men, almost a separate species. An office worker or shopkeeper worked all day in comfort, relaxed with friends or hobbies in the evening, then retired to sleep in a comfortable bed, snug and secure. But seamen led hard, sometimes dangerous lives, and unless they swallowed the hook, rarely lived long enough to collect a pension. In a slow tub like the *Rembrandt* they could spend thirty days at sea without seeing a women or having a drink; and in that respect shipboard life answered to Dr Johnson's observation that it resembled existence in a prison. But once ashore, and compensating for their imbalanced mode of life by drinking too much, they were at the mercy of diseased women, confidence tricksters and knife-flicking wharf-rats, creatures of the shadows who preyed on solitary seamen as they meandered back to their ship, sometimes never reaching it. It was no life for the unmarried young: in a general freighter picking up charters as she went along, a trip could last upwards of a year. This would be followed by a hectic leave, which is not the most favourable occasion for selecting a lifetime partner. But when youth gave place to the middle years, with perhaps the decease of parents and the break-up of the family home, there would be few marriageable women either available or willing to share the remainder of their lives. Eventually, for those who survived, there would be no place to go except the Flying Angel missions and, finally, the homes for retired seamen.

As the months passed and port succeeded port, my Presbyterian morality was modified by a gradual understanding of these things, and I came to accept the captain's double standards. He knew the men were raiding the cargo: but in ports where no money was issued because of currency restrictions, he was also aware that the crew were not going ashore penniless simply to admire the local sights. He complained heatedly of their behaviour to the officers, but he did not inform the dock police, for that would have led to arrests and the depletion of his crew. He was too paternalistic for that. Newport had been an exception; or possibly he didn't consider the firemen there to be true seamen.

However, there was one port we sailed into where his protective attitude faltered.

8

Marie Celeste II

The chief steward, without knowing it, had the instincts of a
Bohemian. He lived for the day. In the matter of catering
administration, this took the form of a regime of feasts and
famines, but it was some time before we recognized this aspect
of his temperament. While we wandered about the Mediterranean, from Palestine to Greece, thence to Algeria and back to
Egypt, we were hardly aware of this eccentricity and his secret
was safe. But when we had negotiated the Suez Canal and
sailed down the Red Sea, with its burning dawns and sunsets,
on our way to Aden, the alternations of our diet became
apparent, and painfully so on the longer trips to Australia and
Canada and beyond.

In port, dinners were sumptuous seven-course affairs, after
which Minto and I would take digestive tablets and lie groaning
on our bunks for an hour or so. After a week or two at sea the
courses would dwindle steadily until three was the most you
could expect, one of which was bound to be chilled melon. The
other two courses were composed of variously disguised
concoctions of dehydrated cabbage and equally dehydrated
potatoes, with no meat at all. The substantial items of food had
all been used up. And when in a sickly condition we arrived at
the next port, back would come the banquets.

Yet our digestive systems managed to cope with the erratic
burdens imposed on them with an adaptability that might have
been educational to dieticians – until, that is, we reached Aden
and took on a supply of fresh water. But 'fresh' was the last
thing you could say about Aden water. It looked like cold tea but
tasted infinitely worse. It was brackish and evil-smelling, and

imparted its disgusting flavour to every liquid for which it was used – tea, coffee, and the lime-juice that was drunk ritualistically at all meals. It was held by Wainwright, the second sparks, who had studied archaeology before the war, that the reservoirs of Aden, which had reputedly been constructed by Nebuchadnezzar, were still being used, and that they hadn't been cleaned out since the fall of Babylon. We could well believe it.

What was even worse, Aden was short of food, and there were to be no feasts in that inhospitable place of mountain and desert. Even the Royal Navy pilot requested a couple of white loaves, for which he was prepared to waive his dues. His request was refused, but this may have had to do with an incident when we were approaching the port by the zigzag lanes of buoys which guided us to the harbour.

By this time I had been put on a watch. I was taking my trick at the wheel when a large dhow crowded to the gunwhales with crew, passengers and, some said, slaves, bore down on us from two points on the starboard bow. The attention of the pilot was drawn to the oncoming vessel but he seemed unconcerned and gave no instructions to slacken speed or alter course. It is possible he had downed a few chota pegs before he came aboard. The second mate tried to conceal his agitation, but his was as nothing compared with the frightful clamour coming from the natives on the dhow.

Any schoolboy knows that steam gives way to sail, and apparently the Arabs thought so, for they did not turn about or drop the huge yard with its striped close-hauled sail.

'Not to worry, old boy. Those dhows can turn on a sixpence, don't you know,' he confided to a very pale second mate.

Collision seemed inevitable: then with a fraction of a second to go, the dhow gybed, almost scraping the paint from our quarter. It was a superb display of seamanship, and how the native craft had brought it off, when its deck was invisible for the swarm of frantic, yelling Arabs milling about in all directions like an upset hive of bees, was more than we could understand. Perhaps Allah had intervened. But it was no thanks to the pilot, and he did not get his white loaves.

Before I was much older I had reason to remember that occasion, when another collision seemed imminent, although the circumstances were curiously different. We were bound for Lourenço Marques in Mozambique, then known as Portuguese

East Africa. By then the combination of Aden water and the chief steward's whimsical catering methods had begun to take effect. The dehydrated vegetables mixed with the water produced a noxious paste of indescribable ghastliness, as unsightly as it was unpalatable. It also produced nausea, dysentery and boils, massive tumescent lumps on necks and arms that kept one awake at nights, and which, by a freakish process of justice, it was the chief steward's task to dress. His nursing qualifications were doubtful, and it was rumoured by his victims that he had taken a first-aid course in an abattoir; so adding injury to the insult to their gastronomy. Truly were the Arabs revenged.

In broken weather these problems might have been serious, but it was May and we were sailing through equatorial waters. The sun blazed from a sky white with heat glare on a sea that was like a polished disc of blinding steel, its surface riffled only by a flight of flying fish or school or dolphins. Awnings had been spread over the spars of the poop and the boat-decks, and under them the off-watch crew lolled and drowsed, wrote sweat-stained letters, lazily did their *dhobi* or played cribbage.

The nights too were hot, so I tried my hand at making a hammock. It was not a success. I cadged some sailcloth, a palm-and-needle and some brass eyelets from Chippy, and got to work. I folded the ends of the sailcloth and sewed them up with sail-twine, hammering brass eyelets into the folds and stretching cords through them. The finished article looked neat and seamanlike and, not without pride, I took my handiwork up to the boat-deck and rigged it between a davit and a cleat on the bulkhead. Gingerly I lowered myself into its rough embrace and settled back, already anticipating the delights of sleeping under the stars. There was a harsh tearing sound as the eyelets were ripped from the canvas, and I landed heavily on the deck. A shout of laughter from down aft indicated that not everyone was dozing in the shade.

A jolt of a different kind was in store. I was at the wheel, late on the morning watch, when it happened. The third mate had gone below for a spell, perhaps for an early lunch or maybe to tend his boils, and I was alone on the bridge. This was against regulations, but discipline was relaxed in the *Rembrandt*, we were literally in the doldrums, and we had sighted nothing but fish for a week. The radio officers were becoming neurotic from idleness and killed time tuning in to remote stations.

No sooner had the third left the outside world to the flying fish and myself, than I was seized by acute gastric torment owing, I suppose, to my last glass of lime-juice diluted by Aden water. Hardly aware of what I was doing, I stumbled from the wheelhouse to the wing of the bridge and retched violently over the side for a couple of long sweating minutes.

When I had recovered a little, I staggered back to the wheel and corrected the course which had veered while I had been away, proving the existence of a fairly strong current. Then I saw the ship for the first time, hardly more than a speck on the horizon, like a mote on a lens, on that flawless sea. It was right ahead.

The third mate had warned me to ring the ship's bell in the unlikely event of my sighting anything, but I had been conning up on Articles 18 and 19 of the steering and sailing rules, and I knew that I should keep the oncoming vessel on my port. So I eased the wheel gently to starboard. She was about ten miles off and I saw no reason for disturbing the third's lunch, or whatever else he was doing.

Just then two different types of flying fish broke surface simultaneously. The first group were the size of thrushes and skimmed low across the water like a shower of equidistant arrows, their fin-beats so rapid they blurred in the light. The other type was blue-backed, as long as herrings, and they shot out of the sea like rockets at random intervals, reaching as high as the yard-arms before gliding downwards in slow graceful swallow-dives. With some reluctance I turned from the performance to check the position of the other ship. I was surprised to see her still above the fo'c'sle-head, only much nearer, and I guessed she was bearing down pretty fast.

Again I put the wheel over a bit and straightened on course, and I made a resolution that if Moby Dick himself showed up I would not take my eyes from this strangely manoeuvring vessel.

It was a sensible decision, for again the ship veered over to her port so that she remained right ahead. It was as though a magnetic force were irresistibly drawing us together, although later I realized she must have been moving in a curve at the will of the current. And moving very fast indeed.

I began sweating again, but not from nausea. There was a mnemonic jingle we were taught at nautical college: 'Green to green, red to red; perfect safety, go ahead.' Which applied to lights, but the same rule held good for daylight hours. This meant that if your ship's starboard was likely to pass the same side on the other ship, there was no problem. But there were no jingles to assist in the present case; and though I recited Articles 18 and 19 at top speed, I could find no helpful course of action in them either.

Yet despite my rising anxiety, I was glad of the chance to practise seamanship in a real situation with no college lecturers or experienced officers on hand to intervene and criticize. I knew I had to get the port side of the *Rembrandt* in line with that of the other ship, so I wrenched the wheel hard over and watched the bows gather momentum and slowly lumber round to starboard until I had the other ship heading for our beam. She was then about quarter of a mile off, and it would have been far too late to summon the third mate in time to avert a collision. I could see by her superstructure she was a well-founded Portuguese liner of about 20,000 tons displacement, and she was licking through the water as though her sole purpose in life was to ram stray merchantmen.

Then, when the moment seemed right, I reversed the wheel hard over to port so as to bring our stern round and clear of the rogue liner's direction of travel. With about a cable's length to go I straightened on course until the two vessels were now parallel and passing each other, but with little to spare.

It was then that I became aware of the hubbub below. My exertions at the wheel hadn't gone unnoticed. We had heeled badly, and the crew were shaken abruptly out of their torpor in time to see a large passenger ship in dangerous proximity. The next minute the third and the chief mate came quivering to a halt before me and I was getting the bawling-out of a lifetime. It was thoroughly deserved but I hardly listened, for by then the liner was passing us, and what I saw made me point incredulously in her direction. The officers paused in their abuse and turned to stare at the ship that had almost ended the SS *Rembrandt*'s career. And mine.

As she went by, and other crew members swear to the truth of this, there wasn't a soul to be seen; no seamen leaning on the rails, no passengers lounging on the boat-decks, no officers parading the bridge and, what gave us the nastiest shock of all, no helmsman in the wheelhouse. . . . The ship was deserted, so

far as we could see. The chief sparks morsed out the traditional
interrogation when ships pass each other – *What ship, where
bound?* – but without response; so there was no one in the
wireless-room either.

It must have been one of the captain's two-bottle days, for my
manoeuvres and the shouts from the crew hadn't wakened him,
which spared the third mate and me some awkward explanations. Boils and nausea would not, as Nicholls's *Seamanship and
Nautical Knowledge* has it, have *exonerated* us from our respective
departures from accepted procedure. And since the taint of
malpractice also pervades upwards, the mate decided that the
Old Man had enough worries to contend with, so he wouldn't
add to them. The sparks were to warn shipping in the area, if
any, and he would make some discreet inquiries when we got to
Lourenço Marques. Meanwhile the less said about the business,
the better.

In fact we debated the matter for days. Had plague struck
down the entire ship's company? Unlikely, we thought,
considering the speed of the vessel. Or had mutiny broken out,
followed by general mayhem, with a Portuguese Mr Christian
taking his followers in the lifeboats to a better existence
somewhere? Again, a skeleton crew could hardly have raised
enough steam for the rate of travel. And what about the absent
helmsman?

Wainwright's theory was typically urbane: 'My guess is that
they'd taken on a supply of Aden water. Latin stomachs not
used to the grim but strengthening ordeal of British cooking,
they simply succumbed to the wretched stuff!'

Mr Gregan offered a more practical explanation: 'Probably
they were all just having a siesta in their cabins. The officer on
watch might have been in the chart-room, and with him out of
the way, the helmsman could have sat cross-legged on the floor
still keeping a hold on the wheel. You can do this once you've
got the measure of the current.'

It seemed to me the current had taken control of the liner, but
it was true what the mate said, for I had done it myself on the
midnight watch when fatigue had got the better of me. There
was a box containing an Ordis signalling light in the corner of
the wheelhouse which was very convenient for the purpose. I
would doze off and wake up to see a different set of
constellations from those on which I had closed my eyes. The

second mate strolled in while I was getting back on course on one occasion and issued the standard rebuke: 'I don't mind you writing your name on the ocean, but please don't go back to stroke the Tee....'

It was as well we never came near another ship with a helmsman thus disengaged, particularly if it was a latter-day *Marie Celeste*.

9

Marguerite

We docked at two ports in Mozambique, and in retrospect a casual visitor might have considered Beira the more friendly of the two, being more spontaneous and *African*. Even the cathedral there, whose matin bells rang across the river, had a tinge of earth colour showing through its whiteness. The Lourenço Marques cathedral, though architecturally superior, was encased with an icy marble that hurt the eye by day and presented a spectral appearance at night.

Beira was a leisurely place. The graceful manoeuvres of the flamingos, the ambling Zulu stevedores, the alcoholic tally clerks, and even the bulbous flying boat that swooshed down on the river most mornings, all shared a lazy attitude to life in that town on the edge of the interminable bush. Melons swelled in the sun on roofs and verandas. At the riverside native women joked and sang as they laundered their linen by beating them on flat stones.

There was no singing in Lourenço Marques. It was a handsome town with profusions of tropical blooms tumbling over walls and adorning the public gardens. At the centre there were ample signs of wealth and prestige, of civil and ecclesiastical authority, all testifying to assumptions of European hegemony. Yet there was a brooding watchfulness about the place that seemed covertly hostile. But it was not there that the power and intolerance of Portuguese colonialism revealed itself, but in Beira. As seamen do the world over, some firemen and deck-hands got drunk one night and made their way to the red-light district. With a timing that suggested the raid was prearranged, the police moved in, wielding heavy clubs, the officers carrying pistols. The seamen were at their most defenceless. They were quickly rounded up and thrown into the local gaol. In the morning Captain Davis was informed that if he wanted to see his crew again they would be discharged on payment of the equivalent in escudos of ten pounds sterling per head. A large sum in those days. With an unwonted meekness that diminished his reputation as a domineering paternalist, the captain paid up, and subsequently logged the money from the men's pay-off.

To be fair to him, it is doubtful if any British commander would have acted differently, but a few days later a victory boat pulled in and it was seen how the Americans handled the problem. Confronted with what seems to have been a standard ultimatum, the captain of that vessel promptly armed the officers with rifles and the men with weapons of their choice – baseball bats, marlinspikes, cargo hooks – and marched them off in a body to storm the gaol and liberate their comrades. This accomplished, pandemonium ensued, and the celebrations lasted till daybreak.

That was how these matters should be dealt with, we thought, with a respect bordering on envy. It was obvious that drunk seamen were the victims of an official conspiracy, and that the police were practising a form of the badger game, using the lure of the brothels to arrest men and demand ransom for them.

Brownlees and Griffiths tried to organize reprisals but enthusiasm was lacking. The men had no firearms, their bruises still ached, and they had little relish to renew acquaintance with the gaol, which had no bunks in the cells and where cockroaches as big as mice crawled over them all night as they lay on the mud floor nursing their wounds.

It wasn't until the Fiji Isles that I came to know something about the night life of prisons; but I didn't have so long to wait for a visit to a brothel. It arose out of a misunderstanding.

After Mozambique we retraced our course to the Mediterranean, stopping at Greece before sailing to Algiers, that lovely hybrid city on a hillside which combined Parisian elegance with Moorish obliquity. A high-spirited sparks from a neighbouring ship had led a party of junior officers ashore one night. I had tagged along at their invitation without the least notion of where we were going. The names *Moulin Rouge* and *Chat du Noir* meant nothing to me, and I supposed they were street cafés such as lined the broad palm-bordered avenues of the French part of town. But we left the well-lit streets with their throngs of smartly dressed women and strolling *boulevardiers*, and entered the whitewashed warren that was the kasbah. At the far end of each twisting lane, at the top of every winding flight of steps, a hooded Arab stood lurking as though in wait for the solitary tourist. Seeing our numbers, they melted into the shadows at our approach. The sparks had come armed with a Very pistol and some cartridges, and as we passed through a tiny square fragrant with magnolia and lemon trees he fired off a round over the heads of a group of Arabs. There was an echoing explosion and a vivid burst of green light that filled the square and blotted out the stars. When darkness rushed in again and the starlight returned, the Arabs had understandably made themselves scarce.

Chuckling at his easy victory, the sparks related other, more serious encounters in the Arab quarter, until he stopped at a large house decorated in the Moorish style, and tapped at the door. A panel slid back and unseen eyes glinted at us, weighing us up. The sparks hid the Very pistol in his jacket. The door swung open and we passed into a dimly lit vestibule, where we were scrutinized more closely by a gigantic Negro wearing a red turban, and a silk-clad concierge-type woman of middle age. The inspection apparently to their satisfaction, we were ushered towards a beaded screen, at the side of which sat an old crone with a face like pumice-stone. She stuck out a grey claw and someone dropped a few centimes into it.

I realized we were not in a restaurant, but since no one had enlightened me about the true function of the place, I thought we must be in a gambling den and, stepping through the screen, I half expected to see rows of tables presided over by sinister croupiers. Instead, we were in a large hall with an internal court surrounded by clustered columns surmounted by intricately decorated arches which reminded me of paintings of the Alhambra. Above the arches were trellised galleries divided by smaller columns which led the eye upwards to a domed ceiling inscribed with calligraphic motifs, probably quotations from the Koran.

I stood there fascinated by the architectural splendour of the place and only gradually realized that it was filled with people –

well-dressed Frenchmen, American servicemen and a few
uniformed seamen like ourselves. And weaving among the men
provocatively clad girls of mixed racial origins chatted and
laughed and generally made themselves agreeable. An air of
discreet animation pervaded the scene, as though a tasteful sort
of party were in progress. Now and then a couple would
disappear through an arched doorway in an alcove. Behind a
colonnade stood a cocktail bar where my companions were
already ordering cognac. It was all so like a Hollywood version
of a caliph's party that if Bob Hope and Bing Crosby had come
wisecracking into our midst, it would have seemed perfectly
natural.

The illusion was sustained when I was introduced to a girl
called Elise who might well have been a stand-in for Dorothy
Lamour. At the thought of what this delightful person was, my
schoolboy's French petrified on my tongue under waves of
conflicting emotions, chief of which were embarrassment,
prudishness and an absurd desire to appear a man of the world,
an ambition that was brusquely shattered by Riley, the fourth
engineer who burred: 'Jock's a virgin, mam'selle. Does he get it
for half price?'

She laughed prettily: *'Hélas, M'sieur, c'est pas possible. Quel
dommage. . . .'*

I studied the Moorish decor and sipped my cognac. *'Mon ami
il est maboul,'* I muttered, rigid with mortification. But for several
reasons, one vital part of me was not rigid at all. Elise was not
unlike some of the smarter female members of my tennis club.
Even her gauzy skirt resembled tennis shorts, the better to show
off her shapely legs. It was impossible to imagine such a
charmingly normal person trading her flesh for cash. But a more
powerful dampener of passion was the expression I had seen on
the face of a seaman that morning, a look of rueful despair and
infinite sadness. He had been diagnosed as an advanced
syphilitic and was being sent home.

For the first time in my life I got drunk that night, which of
course didn't take me very long. My shipmates were just
beginning to enjoy themselves, so the Madame provided me
with an escort to guide my rubbery steps back to the *Rembrandt*.
His name, I think, was Ahmed, and to repay him for his trouble
I gave him a few francs and an extempore lecture on the evils of
drink all the way to the ship. Since he was a Muslim, I could

have saved my reeking breath.

My main resistance to Elise's allurements, however, came
from quite another cause than either puritanism or stricken
seamen. While we were at Piraeus, I had met a girl in the train
from Athens where I had been sightseeing. The carriage was
crowded and I rose to give her my seat, a reflex courtesy that
seemed to astonish the other passengers. Maybe centuries of
Turkish domination had obliged the Greeks to regard women as
social inferiors. Or maybe they were like that anyway. But I
could regard Marguerite only with the greatest enchantment,
and her dark, colourful beauty and the warmth of her smile
might have given my home-bred manners an extra spur.

At the station she thanked me in a mixture of English and
French, languages she happened to be studying at her last year
of school. From that moment, in the hesitant fashion of youth, a
tender friendship was born which we soon imagined was love.
Each evening we walked through the squares and gardens of
Athens, then a shabby but romantic town. From the Acropolis
the view in all directions, from the serrated mountains to the sea
of kingfisher blue, pained the heart with its clear, piercing
beauty as it stirred the mind with evocations of history and
legend.

All too soon the warm, moon-haunted evenings, fragrant
with blossom and citrus trees, dwindled to our poignant
leave-taking. Nothing formal was established between us, but
an attachment such as ours could have only one logical and
natural conclusion – I would return some day and meet her
parents and we should never be parted again.

As we strolled to the harbour the music of bouzoukis
thrummed in the tavernas, lightening our solemn mood. The
unquenchable spirit of the Greeks was struggling to the surface
after the years of subjection and famine, the essential *romiosini*
unimpaired. The music and the restored gaiety of the cafés gave
us the illusory hope that life would not be so cruel as to keep us
apart for long. The Greek word for it was *kairos*: we had seized
the fateful moment, and we were ready to commit ourselves to
the fulfilment of a common destiny. Or so we thought at the
time, never doubting the durability of our love. After many
garlic-flavoured kisses, I left for the ship sensing that my life
was about to assume a responsible shape.

The first of her letters arrived in Kalamata, our next port of call, and when I opened the flimsy but fat envelope the tiny petals of a yellow blossom fell from the pages in a golden shower to the cabin floor. She wrote ardently of her love and her longing that we should be reunited at the earliest opportunity; and so on, for page after page, barely managing to cram into the last paragraph that she had spoken of our attachment to her parents.

In Algiers another letter awaited me with the same delicate cargo of mimosa blossom, amorous sentiments and an almost offhand reference to her family. Her sisters, whom I had met, sent their fondest regards, and her parents hoped that I was well. Despite my deep affection for Marguerite, I got the impression of a slowly forming net, lighter than gossamer, stretching out towards me over the sea and over my future. I was both flattered and alarmed.

A third letter arrived the morning after the visit to the bordello, a morning of unaccountable pains in the head and grittiness in the eyeballs. I had become weary of Minto's amusement at Marguerite's floral tributes, so I took the letter and my hangover out on deck. My brain reeled in the onshore breeze, and the sound of the ripping envelope rasped my nerves. 'My darling monomarakimou,' she began, 'I pray for the time when we are together again. . . .' After a few pages another strand of gossamer reached out, this time more like an invisible tentacle: 'My father wishes you his best memories, and wonders when you will be chief officer on your ship, *mon petit chou*. . . .' The last of the blossom whirled away.

I leant on the deck-rail and groaned. My foot was hardly on the first rung of the ladder and already her parents were sketching in the salient features of my career. The family was 'respectable', and naturally they were concerned about Marguerite's future welfare. But I wasn't sure if I had intended our courtship to progress quite so rapidly. There was no denying the sincerity of my feelings towards their daughter, but under the patina of moonlight in a blossom-filled ancient city a discussion of practical issues would have been a kind of sacrilege. So without realizing it, I had been dallying with the emotions of a young lady. I had been serious at the time, of course, but now I looked ahead, and unless we returned to Athens, which seemed unlikely, I shouldn't see her again for years. Could I retain my burning passion for that long? It seemed doubtful. A young seaman has no means of knowing what awaits him in the next port, and therein lies its excitement and adventure. I was also in love with the sea.

Meanwhile what would Marguerite's parents say if they knew that their prospective son-in-law had visited a brothel and got horribly drunk, in the one night? It was obvious that I was not quite ready for matrimony. And as I thought of its ramifications, I recoiled at the prospect of becoming anything remotely like the corpulent Mr Gregan or the two-bottle-a-day Captain Davis. Then I remembered the months and years of separation endured by my own parents. My mother had been a patient martyr to a seafaring family tradition, a way of life for many women when she was young. But now the flicker of a new doubt glanced across my mind to join the others. Could I subject my future wife to years of intermittent loneliness, and possibly sexual frustration, to say nothing of my own? Life was getting complicated.

The breeze was carrying small clouds over the town, and their shadows raced over the jumble of white terraces as they stepped downhill to the blue waters of the harbour and the bays. Algiers was by far the loveliest port at which we had so far docked; and there were many cities and lands all over the world I had yet to see. Marriage could wait. I was seventeen years old and the cook had declared we were bound for South Australia. Who would want to look further ahead than that? I would write to Marguerite and explain, as gently as I could, the insuperable difficulties confronting a continued relationship, and leave it to her good sense to draw its own conclusions. So I mused, leaning on the rail.

Just then, a French woman of middle years came staggering along the quayside, much as I had done myself accompanied by Ahmed. She was singing a jaunty air in a drunken, raucous voice. Her clothes were filthy and dishevelled. A few deck-hands up for'ard stopped work to watch her progress. Suddenly she stopped at the edge of the quay, lifted her bedraggled skirt and urinated into the harbour. One of the men gasped slightly and gave an embarrassed laugh. She looked up: 'Alors, matelot! Comment ça va! You like zhig-zhig, eh?'

No one responded to the invitation, which shouldn't have surprised her. But she made an obscene gesture to the man, following it up with a volley of demotic abuse, apparently bitterly offended that nobody wanted to avail themselves of her fading charms. *'Va te faire foutre!'* she rasped, then resumed her zigzag course down the quay.

My nature and upbringing had led me to believe that women were in a special category, beings of subliminal power more fundamentally connected with the essence of life than the male of the species. And my experience with Selima had confirmed that they possessed the immediate key to metaphysical realms, unapproachable otherwise except by mystics and visionaries. The horror I felt, therefore, at seeing this forlorn ruin of a creature teetering irretrievably downhill, though still clinging to the remains of a wry courage, cannot easily be imagined. That I was able to retain a vestige of my former reverence for her sex was due mainly to the memory of Marguerite's pure character and delicate beauty. Only chance could bring us together again, but I should never forget her.

10

Australia Bound

We cast off from Algiers and made our way to Bône, further along the coast, for a cargo of phosphates. The ship sailed light, which was bad, for we ran straight into a ferocious gale and there was no time for marital speculations. The helmsman could do little to control the course but keep her head-on to the onslaught while the empty vessel rolled and twirled like a mad drunk. Worse, the elderly engines chose this time to break down and soon we were drifting dangerously close to an unknown lee shore. An experienced able seaman was instructed to take soundings with a hand-lead, the only occasion I saw this done. It was nearly dusk, and how the man could distinguish between the soiled bits of rag, linen, bunting and so on, which denoted the intervals of depth, was a mystery to the younger hands. Allowing for the slight weigh, he heaved the lead for'ard, paying out an estimated length of line. When this was vertical the lead was dropped till the sea-bed was touched. Immediately it was hauled up and a reading made which he called out in the howling wind to the bridge.

'By the deep eight . . .'

'By the mark seven . . .'

'A quarter less seven. . . .'

It was time to drop anchors. The coastal cliffs loomed ominously. Steam was turned on and the windlass made ready with the mate in charge and Chippy manipulating the brakes. The heel of the lead revealed that we were over a sandy bed, and if the ship had been loaded the odds were that we would have drifted on to a shoal. As it was, the tethered ship swung and tumbled through the night as the engineers struggled to repair the ailing engines.

I couldn't sleep that night for the unaccustomed silence, a sense of helplessness and the fear that the ship might drag anchors on the soft sea-bed. But by dawn the repair work was complete and our course for Bône resumed.

Phosphate is a detestable material, a foul, powdery stuff that sticks to everything including the back of one's throat. So that afternoon a few of us went ashore to rinse away its acrid taste with the local muscatel wine which was sweet, strong and cheap. The owner of the bistro was a hospitable Frenchman and our stay was prolonged. This was unfortunate, for when we finally emerged blinking into the sunlight, we were promptly stoned by a mob of Arabs who may have thought we were French matelots. Argument and remonstrance were useless. We were outnumbered and they were sober. There was no choice but instant flight, and we bundled into the nearest gharry and shouted to the driver to make off as fast as his ancient nag could carry us.

The wine and the heat may have been the cause of some confused directions, for the driver, instead of taking us to the harbour, drove about a mile out of town and stopped at an ornate Catholic church with a smiling priest at the door. Perhaps he had an arrangement with the gharry-wallah. We were invited to enter, but only after a sizeable gratuity had changed hands.

The interior of the place dazed the senses, as I suppose it was meant to do, the décor a brilliant scheme of white and gold, with painted saints in niches, eyes upturned as though expecting rain. A sickly smell of incense hit us like a miasmic wall. I thought of the churches of Scotland I had been used to, in which a vase of seasonal flowers on the altar was the only concession to adornment you were likely to get. But we padded politely after the priest as he pointed out features of interest, a plaster model of the nativity scene, and a few donated paintings showing saints in somewhat histrionic postures of religious enthusiasm. Riley was from Belfast and he was not looking comfortable, but he held himself in check until we returned to the portico where stood a marble statue which appeared to have lost its big toes, as though by gangrene. We turned inquiringly to our guide. This, he explained in French, was due to the humble devotion of the faithful. And he smiled with simple pride.

We looked blank, and Riley enlightened us: 'The papist means that the dupes have kissed the fock'n things away!'

'Oh,' we said, and left, the Ulsterman the first to board the gharry which had waited for us.

On the way back, about half a mile from this opulent church, we passed what at first had seemed the town refuse dump, but which on closer inspection proved to be a collection of wretched hovels of canvas and corrugated iron. A stench arose from the place that was nothing like incense. It was indeed a refuse area, but for people, rejects from Western colonialism. Black-clothed women did things with pans and reeds, stunted children crawled between the shacks, and the few men about sat staring miserably into vacancy as though wondering why the Prophet had forbidden suicide. And this social running sore was within sight of a church whose founder had reputedly said: 'Blessed are the meek: for they shall inherit the earth.' Theirs was the meekness of the totally abject, but they looked far from being blessed.

It was not surprising that the Arabs occasionally threw stones at Europeans. Some day it was conceivable they might throw something worse.

At Port Said our carpenter saw his last landfall. An Australian charter might prolong the trip indefinitely, and the old man was overdue for retirement. Few could have earned it more. Chippy had spent a lifetime at sea, which had spanned his apprenticeship on a windjammer to the advent of the steam turbine and jet propulsion, his career coinciding with more changes in the means of travel than all previous innovations since man first used a log to cross a river. Watching the old shellback stump down the gangway with tool-case in one hand, sea-bag over his shoulder, pipe jutting from his leathery face, was like witnessing the incarnate end of an era. Now we were entering a new age, and the fresh-faced product of a technical school and evening classes who had been flown out to replace Chippy was just as representative of it as Chippy was of the age of sail.

The new man, Hollins by name, had been the leading tenor of the local choir in his North Country home town; and he had come to sea equipped not merely with a certificate to prove his technical proficiency, but with a repertoire of sea-shanties. These he would render at ever opportunity with what he supposed was an authentic rollicking breeziness, which embarrassed everyone within earshot. The crew loved to sing, especially in taverns ashore, but nobody ever sang sea-shanties. Old Chippy had obliged the company with 'Blow the Man Down' occasionally, but he had remembered it as a work song from his early days. And now Chippy was gone.

A more serious aspect of the newcomer was suggested by a deck-hand who had sailed with the man on his first trip; a matter concerning the loss of an anchor and cable off Gibraltar, and this was to have curious repercussions in Australia.

Another addition to the crew was obtained less conventionally after we had negotiated the Suez Canal and left Port Taufiq astern against a sky like a scarlet banner. The cabin-boy, a notorious scrounger always on the look-out for stray articles of clothing, discovered a pair of jeans under some dunnage in the for'ard locker. Clutching what he could see of his prize, he gave a heave, and found it contained the legs of our first stowaway.

Dusty Miller proved to be a Cockney able seaman who had jumped his homeward-bound vessel and stolen aboard the *Rembrandt* at Port Said when he learnt that her destination was Australia. Family problems were the cause of the switch, he explained to the captain. But when we knew him better, we surmised that England with its ration books and national insurance, its grey weather and tight restrictions, was not the place for such a man. Seafaring had taught him the scope of the world and the measure of his own resources. If Chippy was the epitome of a bygone age, Dusty was the archetypal image of a more timeless character; the vagabond and wanderer of independent mind, stopping where his fancy took him, up-anchoring if things got stale or if the mood to roam seized him again. But his papers were in order, and since we were short of a deck-hand owing to the departure of the man who had loved women too incautiously, he was signed on and appointed to the same watch as mine.

This was fortunate in several respects. He was a capable seaman, an interesting companion off watch and, more particularly, he possessed a genuine if erratic taste in literature. His schooling had been brief, so his opinions were self-formed and, because of this, clearly expressed. Keats, for instance, was a flawed genius who wasted his talents on describing in flowery hyphenated terms nature which he imperfectly understood, and scenes of classical mythology which were merely escapist fantasies from the horrors of his work at the surgery. Tennyson was superior because he made use of classical allusions, in peoms such as 'The Lotus-Eaters', to illuminate eternal pre-occupations of the human spirit. Byron was great because of his verve and impatience with hypocritical morality, but his egoism kept showing through the fancy dress he assumed in such roles as Don Juan and Childe Harold. Dusty's Bible, and the most valued of his few possessions, was a copy of Palgrave's *Golden Treasury of Verse*, and this he lent me, correctly suspecting gaps in my own literary awareness.

Another boost to my tardy intellectual growth on that long trip was provided by a group who met in the chief engineer's cabin before dinner for sundowners. Minto and I shared a cabin in the engineers' alleyway, and almost every evening a bell-like, ringing tone resonated along its length and entered the cabins. This was produced by the chief's rubbing a finger dipped in pink gin round the edge of a wine glass, and it never failed to rouse the inhabitants of the alleyway from their torpor. Soon, the guests in smart tropic whites or khaki drill had arranged themselves round the large cabin, and drinks were served. Conversation was civilized and urbane for the most part, the subjects ranging from art and literature to philosophy and politics – the latter inevitably, since all but the fourth engineer were socialists. I formed the impression that had it not been for the war, some of them would certainly have become lecturers at university departments of engineering at least, for the debates were frequently scholarly and finely argued, or so it seemed to me. I could not resist comparing their breadth of culture with that of the mates, particularly Mr Gregan, whose conversation under similar conditions was usually confined to an exchange of nautical anecdotes. Fascinating though some of these were, an evening spent in their company left me with a sensation of disappointed expectation, like going to a banquet and being served with nothing but *hors-d'oeuvres*. I had begun to crave for solid argument, and this was provided in abundance by the engineers.

The chief engineer, Thorpe, was a powerfully built man whose complexion matched the pink gins he favoured and who never travelled without an extensive library. I was permitted to borrow freely from its treasures: Wells, Shaw, Marx, Balzac, and so forth, until quite soon my attachment to Nicholls's *Seamanship* slackened off, and the problems of oblique spherical trigo-nometry rapidly lost their appeal. And on look-out duty at nights, instead of reciting the Articles relating to the Rules of the Road, I found myself chanting the poems of Shelley, especially if the moon was spreading a trail of silver over the waves.

Paradoxically my feelings for the seafaring life intensified at this time, and I believed that no other calling under the sun could equal it. As for my ship, I had come to regard her with emotional affection. Other ships might be more graceful or in better trim, but few vessels that I had seen seemed to have such a sturdy and harmonious relationship of parts. When on the second trip her pre-war colours were restored, she became invested with a rudimentary glamour and I wouldn't have changed places with a Conway cadet on the *Queen Mary*. And instead of tedious Atlantic crossings, we were bound for Australia.

11

The Discovery

One morning I came out on deck and gaped at the world, for it seemed that sky, sea and ship had formed a living organism, a visible entity of dancing colours and sunlight and shadow playing on the gently swaying bows. Spindrift broke over the fo'c'sle, scattering jewels of light on the foredeck, and the rigging was a stringed instrument stirred into music by the wind. I was conscious of an elemental joy and wanted to laugh out loud.

Minto was standing nearby, noticing my state of dazed elation. 'You'll get used to all this,' he said. 'Then it'll be nothing but tedium. Same jobs at the same time, every bloody day for years, till you get a super's job if you're lucky. Even the ports will seem the same after a while.'

I had to admit that sightseeing was not the first thing the crew had in mind when they stepped ashore, but I was sure I should be different, that each new landfall would always bring prospects of adventure and new experiences. I said as much. 'And how,' I asked him, waving my arm about, 'could anyone ever tire of this – this extraordinary beauty. This. . . .' Words failed me.

'Rubbish,' he said. 'You'll get blasé. Everyone does. I guarantee before the trip's over you'll get so bored you'll even write poetry.'

'Poetry!' I cried. 'That's ridiculous!'

'I'm telling you. I wrote a poem myself once. I'll show it you. . . .'

That anyone so level-headed as Minto could write poems defied belief; yet when I read his effort, it wasn't at all bad. The theme concerned a look-out on the graveyard watch seeing stars drown in the flood of dawn, and if the rhymes were pedestrian, the ideas were crisply expressed and the scansion was good.

'Why don't you write others?' I asked.

He shrugged and changed the subject, like one who had only performed an exercise to prove he could do it. A repetition of the feat would be superfluous, like reclimbing Everest or ballooning across the Sahara a second time. He had written his poem and that was that.

I was to learn that my cabin mate and I differed in that respect. Whether it was to fulfil his prophecy, or the influence of Dusty's Palgrave and the chief's library, I'm not sure, but the next time I was at the wheel I found myself conjuring up images and rhymes, and assembling them into verses. The sea was like molten glass and no effort was needed to maintain the course, which allowed me to concentrate on this new and engrossing pastime.

After dinner I sat down to write my first poem, an impression of my former village home. Lowering clouds rushed from sheltering hills, gusty rain needled down cobbled streets and over shining roofs; folk with collars turned up hurried homewards to lighted rooms and warm firesides. I think it ended with a moral, something to do with the quiet delights of a well-ordered community in country places. Now this was strange because a lust for travel had enabled me to turn my back on such a life without regrets. So I came to realize, with the help of one of the chief's books on psychology, that my subconscious had spoken, voicing preferences at odds with those of my everyday self.

I had made a discovery. The ship was heading for Australia, for me an unknown land, with the promise of other *terrae incognitae* beyond, but I had stumbled upon the existence of somewhere far more mysterious and strange. And it lay submerged beneath my thoughts, separated from my normal self by a kind of cerebral membrane which the act of writing poetry had penetrated. Indirectly it was evident too that this other self disapproved of the life to which I had subjected it.

It was as though I had been looking at the passing scene from a railway carriage and, turning aside for a moment, realized I was not alone in the compartment, and that this unsuspected stranger did not share my admiration for the view. What was worse, he would not get off at the next stop. We were to be fellow travellers for as long as the journey lasted.

I tried to learn more of this hidden character, and it was with impatience that I took my turn at the wheel or on look-out, to discover what new ideas and themes it might dislodge in the guise of poetry from its obscure lair.

From then on, my notebooks were used less for nautical or astronomical exercises than for explorations of my inscape by means of verse. As I probed deeper, the flow quickened until a definite pattern emerged: almost all the subject-matter concerned the world of nature, its moods and harmonies, and the creatures who responded to its intricate rhythms. It did not seem to be interested in the sea or ships at all, but the implications of this were concealed until much later. Then it worried me that this uninvited guest, who lived in the basement, so to speak, did not see eye to eye with me on the choice of my career. It may even have resented exile from the sympathetic environment of my country home. It was also possible that, like a child, it enjoyed distraction and was easily bored by the humdrum.

Yet despite Minto's prediction, which had only partly come true, I was not bored in the least in those days. Certainly there were few distractions. Day followed day in a wheeling procession of blistering sunlight, followed by miraculously starry nights. Never had I imagined the sky held so many stars. The absence of humidity and the purity of the atmosphere reduced refraction to almost nothing, so that stars were visible the instant they rose above the horizon – which caused some confusion on look-out duty. I would see a bright light on the sea's flat edge and ring the bell to warn the bridge of an approaching ship – two bells for starboard lights, one bell for port and three for right ahead. The mate on the bridge, who had the advantage of height, could see only a newly risen star. After he had been roused from the chart-room a third time on account of airborne ships of this kind, he demanded to know what the hell I was playing at. I should have waited on the appearance of an accompanying red or green light which are weaker than the white, and so take longer to become visible. So one learns.

An even more incompetent first-tripper was my predecessor who never seemed to learn anything, according to Minto. Apparently, while he was on look-out and nearing a port with seventeen lamp standards along the quayside, he rang the bell that number of times, which brought all hands on deck, convinced that the ship was ablaze from stem to stern.

On that seemingly endless trip, only the sun and the stars blazed with their alternating fires of scorching heat and icy brilliance. The Southern Cross was first seen at Suez. Now other strange constellations swung slowly into view. And the bow waves and the propeller-churned wake threw up even more exotic bursts of luminescent splendour. Yet when the sun spread a sheet of gold over the sea again, all was as before with neither ship nor wisp of coastline nor even a gull to be seen.

After two weeks it was possible to believe that this was the only world there ever was: that we were ensnared in a timeless void, suspended in a sphere of light without past or future, destined to sail for ever towards nowhere on a voyage whose purpose had been lost, had vanished like our fading wake.

Off watch we did what we could to pass the time. The officers took turns at pacing the foredeck in pairs, to and fro, to and fro. Down aft the men played cribbage, or at quoits with rings made from rope; or they had make-do-and-mend sessions, repairing gear and equipment. The bosun, now the very last of the shellbacks, knitted crude socks, jabbing with thick needles at the coarse wool as though it were a first-tripper.

The cabins were hot and stifling at nights so I made another attempt at a hammock, which proved to be more durable than my last effort. I slung it on the boat-deck and slept out at nights, my eyes closing on the pageant of stars and my mind filled with sensations of unutterable peace and contentment such as I have never known, before or since. I made another discovery. If the moon rose while I was asleep, I found that my eyes were crossed in the morning, and I presumed this was due to the satellite's gravitational power. With diffidence I presented my theory at the next engineers' pre-prandial gathering.

'Gravitational fiddlesticks!' snorted the chief, not so much because of the untenable argument of my observation, but because it had been proferred by a junior cadet, the lowest form of animal life, according to Captain Bligh. But others supported me, and a typically protracted debate ensued.

When we had paused for breath and to replenish drinks, Minto said: 'Jock's always coming out with things like that. For instance, in the Medi, he noticed that water in the basin went down the plug-hole clockwise. But in Mozambique it went down anti-clockwise, so he said.'

'Nonsense!' said the chief, who seemed to be irritated by my precocity. 'It entirely depends on the motion of the ship.'

All the same, he rose and filled his wash-hand basin to the brim, then pulled out the plug. The water rushed straight down the hole. 'What did I tell you?' he asked triumphantly. 'That's because the ship's as steady as a rock.'

'But Chief,' the second pointed out, 'at this precise moment, we're passing over the Equator?'

My reputation for scientific discovery, so far as Minto was concerned, was maintained, but the chief refused to concede the point, and he was in a grumpy mood at dinner.

Perhaps the chief's irritability had less to do with precocious cadets than a general mounting of tension which had become almost tangible, and which seemed to increase in ratio to the time spent at sea. Bickering broke out between friends. Serious quarrels were started over trivial causes. It was perilous to complain of the cook's terrible food in his presence. Then, one day, Brownlee and Dusty Miller decided to settle their differences on number five hatch. Until that time, nobody guessed that they had any differences, but since they were two of the biggest men aboard, it seemed wiser to let them get on with it.

As news of the impending fight spread, it began to take on the aspect of a cathartic ritual, a means of relieving the accumulated strains of boredom and frustration. Also it was symbolic that the contestants were drawn from the rival operations of the ship – the deck and the engine-room.

In a heat of more than a hundred degrees Fahrenheit they squared up to each other, the one bronzed from working stripped to the waist, the other with the ivory hue of the stokehold gang. A crowd had gathered silently around the hatch but no bets were made, and this was unusual.

Blood was drawn almost at once, for neither was skilled at defensive tactics, being more used to free-for-alls in taverns and cabarets. Soon mingled blood and sweat coursed down their faces as they circled each other, exchanging vicious blows to body and head. Apart from the grunts and thuds as bare kunckles hit flesh, there was no sound, and this was the most unpleasant feature of the fight. No one from either contingent cheered his champion or applauded a successful punch. The

silence was eerie; and some of the spectators looked away
uncomfortably as though wishing they were somewhere else.

At last Dusty waved his hands from side to side. That's it,
Brownlee, old man,' he said, in a perfectly level voice. 'Let's
leave it at that, eh?'

Brownlee tried to conceal his relief. 'Come on, you bastard,'
he said with assumed aggressiveness, his ludicrous southpaw
weaving the air. 'Nobody ever said I don't finish what I start.'

Waddington jumped up on the hatch and pushed them apart,
which couldn't have been difficult. 'Give over, you lads, before
y'get bloody sunstroke. . . . Now shake on it, will you?'

And they did: the suspense was over, for neither was badly
hurt. Amateur heavyweights, without gloves or rules to restrain
them, can kill without meaning to; and they were both popular
men.

After that the crew settled down to more sedate diversions.
The officers continued to pace the foredeck or play bridge. With
great ingenuity a seaman inserted model brigantines into
bottles; and another stretched cured flying fish on painted
hardboard to adorn his parents' living-room. I filled whole
notebooks with excruciating pastoral odes.

Then one day there was a palpable change, hardly more than
a stir in the air, an alteration in the sky's temper. Some dead
brushwood drifted past the hull, and a frigate bird planed over
the masts. The men became brisker at their tasks, and singing
was heard down aft in the men's quarters. Going-ashore gear
was hung out in the sunlight, and some of the crew submitted
their locks to the ministrations of amateur barbers.

After our weeks spent at sea, the thin line of coast, when it
came, was something of an anticlimax. We had reached the
Antipodes at last, but our immediate reaction was: Is that all?
Surely the largest island in the world should present a more
dramatic outline than this dull, flat coast? It could have been
anywhere.

It was in a sober mood that we crept into Fremantle at dead of
night. But the sobriety was short-lived.

12

New Byzantium

That is no country for old men. The young
In one another's arms . . .

W.B. Yeats

In all, we spent about sixteen months wandering around the coasts and islands of Australasia, but that first stop at Fremantle still occupies a special place in the storehouse of my memory.

After the long trip from Aden, the crew went mad. Australian beer of that period was strong and ice cold, and the men couldn't get enough of it, so that their impact on the quiet streets of the town was like a sort of alcoholic bomb-blast. When we pulled out two days later, replete with stores and fuel, there was hardly a sober man aboard. Preparations for sailing were made with such a drunken gaiety and reckless disregard for safety it was a mystery why no one fell overboard – unless, as the older seamen put it, there was a special providence that looked after children, lunatics and sailors. That providence was busy in Fremantle.

The men swarmed up masts like monkeys, swung on lines like so many Tarzans; battened down hatches and replaced derricks as though performing stunts in a carnival or panto-mime. The tricky operation of releasing back-springs and letting go for'ard and aft created scenes reminiscent of the world of Laurel and Hardy. The officers were little better and mooned about issuing vague instructions which nobody heeded. The man at the wheel responded to the pilot's directions with such carefree imprecision that the wake resembled the trail of a sidewinder snake, and may have created the illusion in the minds of the longshoremen watching the erratic behaviour of the stern that the ship itself was drunk. Even the white-haired Dundonian pilot, a pillar of stoical resourcefulness, began to show signs of alarm. But we cleared the heads, deposited the old man in the launch, and made for the open sea with no harm done.

Earlier at dinner the pilot had annoyed me intensely. He was something of a raconteur and had been entertaining the saloon with anecdotes from his adventurous life before he settled for pilotage. The officers were quick to top up his glass. The warmth of their appreciation and hospitality induced in him a mellow mood, and he turned to me, knowing my place of origin, and said: 'There are two things in life I'm proud of. The first, that I was born in Scotland. The second, that I had the sense to leave the damn place as soon as I conveniently could!'

I didn't wait for their approving laugh to finish, and charged in with a comprehensive defence of our mutual homeland, the superiority of its products, one of which they were presently enjoying, the beauty of its scenery, the richness of its history, and the disproportionately high number of great Scots who had contributed their talents for the benefit of mankind ... and so on, until I had run out of breath.

He merely nodded and gave a sagacious grin, which infuriated me, and I was off again, blind to the warning glance of Mr Gregan. This time I used the comparative method, listing the countries we had visited with some of their less attractive features, the poverty, squalor and disease-ridden wretchedness; the superstition, and the corruption of the authorities. And I dared him to explain to the company in what way Scotland was inferior to any one of them.

'Och, laddie,' he said patiently, 'auld Scotia's had its fair share of those things in its time. But you haven't seen Australia yet. You've only glimpsed a fraction of it, as you might a bonnie quine at a crowded dance.... Wait till you've embraced her entirely, then you'll know what I mean.'

I was silent at this, for I remembered something that made me wish I hadn't spoken so hastily.

Minto and I had been given the day off and, instead of scooping up the local ale as though prohibition were hourly expected, like the rest of the crew, we boarded a bus to Perth, the capital of Western Australia, and were enchanted by the place. It was clean, white and modern but not aggressively so, and the rectangularity of the buildings and thoroughfares was softened by an extravagant abundance of flowering trees and shrubs. The climate was delicious and the townsfolk ambled along the streets and pedestrian malls as though they hadn't a care in the world. The Swan River flowed as serenely as its name. No comparison was possible to its Scottish sister town on the edge of the Highlands which, though handsome, was dark and dour. In the new Perth I had absorbed enough impressions to realize faintly with hindsight what the old pilot might mean. I recalled that in the Scottish town, to settle a feud in bygone times, fifty men each from rival clans lined up in a field known as The Inch, and at a signal began a day-long battle. At sundown they had hacked each other to pieces and only three men were left alive. Nothing so barbarous or gory, no tradition so remorseless in its self-righteousness, was conceivable in the Australian Perth.

Someone, freely translating from Montesquieu, has written: 'Happy the land with no history'. The converse may also be true, for Scotland has too much history. Western Australia fits the aphorism neatly: it has archaeology in remote places, otherwise its story has yet to be written, and the people were relaxed, healthy and hospitable, living very much in the present. But there was an omission from this picture of a prosperous and free community which I came to realize later. Certainly we saw no signs of poverty in Perth, or religious bigotry; nor were there obvious indications of oligarchical divisions of wealth. But we didn't see any Aborigines either. By the time the Dundonian had arrived that problem would have been dealt with or tucked out of sight. The early settlers around Perth had made the area bloom like a garden in a wilderness, but only by depriving the natives of their hunting grounds; and the Aborigines had no effective means of combating armed intruders.

Of all the habitations of aboriginal tribes on earth, only the country of Australia had not experienced continuous invasions before the arrival of Europeans. The natives had no knowledge of gunpowder or organized soldiery, and they must have been as helpless as children whose trust had been abused. They are

one of the oldest tribes in the world, and their wisdom goes back
to the 'dream-time' when the world was in its infancy and man
was at one with its total organism; but they were dispossessed
of their ancient lands and there was nothing their gods or
totems could do about it. I never gazed into the smoky,
protuberant eyes of an Aborigine without thinking: This man
knows more than I do of the secret of creation and the enigma of
human fate.

I had been burrowing deeper into the chief's library and had
begun to think about such matters, particularly on look-out
under a canopy of stars when the relative minuteness of the
world is at its most conspicuous and the question of man's
relevance on it is most open to doubt. A pure Aborigine,
uncontaminated by the white man's values, would not have to
think of these things, since an understanding of them was
integrated into the texture of his being. Yet now he would be
hounded from one territory to another at the whims of stock
exchanges and military requirements. An outcast in his own
land, he would believe that his gods had failed him, or had
imposed dire retribution for long-forgotten crimes.

Most of the Aborigines we came across were of mixed race
and probably believed nothing of the kind, having trouble
enough simply to survive. Shunned by the pure-blooded
Aborigines, they were employed as casual labour in the towns
and farmsteads, and were used to the white man's consolations
of alcohol, radio and second-hand cars. The men tended to be
withdrawn and dispirited, but the girls, who were often very
attractive, were altogether more lively and gregarious, as we
soon discovered.

After leaving Fremantle we reached the port of Wallaroo in
South Australia, there to discharge the hated phosphates. We
docked in the afternoon and, as soon as was possible, a party of
us hurried down the long, empty road to the town in the hope
of getting to the pubs before they closed at six o'clock. The
waves were thundering up the Spencer Gulf from the Great
Bight and a stiff breeze made us keep our heads down, so that a
group of giggling, half-caste girls coming from the town took us
completely by surprise. Instantly the desire for beer was
replaced by a different appetite. We had been at sea for a very
long time, and for me Selima was a distant memory. The brief
Australian dusk was fading but there was sufficient light to

guide us to our choices, and with a minimum of indecision, as though it were a well-rehearsed play, couples were soon wandering over to the beach. I found myself talking to a small nubile girl of my own age who didn't seem at all averse to my suggestion that we sheltered from the wind behind a disused barn that stood nearby. And so did something else.

Our passionate kisses could have but one conclusion, and a consummation to our sudden friendship resulted, as powerful as it was mind shattering. Indistinctly I was aware of her own violent spasms, but my attention was more concerned with an intensity of delight so supreme that it seemed my heart would burst, and that some essential part of me would float away from this corporeal world on wings of ecstasy and never return. . . .

When I opened my eyes after a slow descent to the ordinary world, which unaccountably hadn't altered in any way, I was holding a total stranger in my arms. I didn't even know her name. No, she would not come to town with us, as her family were expecting her, and she was late already. Perhaps we would meet again one day, she said, and left to rejoin her sisters and friends. Soon they went laughing up the road in the gathering darkness, their white skirts blown sideways by the onshore wind. My luminous watch showed that barely twenty minutes had passed, yet my mind still reeled with its recent proximity to a timeless dimension of the world.

It was not surprising that some religions condemned the act outside marriage, for its effects were liberating and anarchic, and it revealed the existence of an infinitely more splendid paradise than the posthumous one promised by clergymen. Theologians may argue that the great mystics had encountered the same place in their own fashion. But mystics were usually old men whose interest in the sublunary route was academic. Australia was a young, vigorous land, so far as Caucasians were concerned, and like Yeat's 'Byzantium', it was no country for old men. The young were often 'in one another's arms', when they were not swimming or surfing, or drinking cold, strong beer and singing sentimental songs.

Some of the crew found these attractions irresistible and jumped ship, and they were written off in the log as deserters. The final urge to quit the sea was frequently provided by a fervid romance in progress; but the real lure was the country itself, its superb beaches, an unaccustomed sense of freedom it imparted, the silent blue distances, the grandeur of the Bush. There was space to manoeuvre for the enterprising or adventurous. One man joined some cattle-drovers he had met in a bar in Port Lincoln; another went north to fish off the Barrier Reef; and a third got a berth as a deck-hand in a schooner that traded in the Pacific islands. They left at night, a sea-bag over a shoulder and with never a thought of the money the company owed to them.

A young seaman fell seriously in love with a local beauty he had met at a dance in Port Pirie, and successfully proposed marriage. Since love seemed a fleeting thing, he was advised against it, but without a word he gathered his few belongings and quietly disappeared. I remember the night he met her because I had taken a girl home from the same dance. Her abode lay miles away from the port, and for hours we trudged across a featureless plain under the stars. At last we arrived at an isolated timber steading, built by her father who was waiting up for her on the veranda, a rifle on his knees. I heard the click of a safety-catch and did not prolong my farewell.

It may have been a coincidence, or the proximity of the Outback where work on the ranches was available, but with the exception of Chippy Hollins when his turn came, our deserters chose to leave at small ports where nothing much happened and the arrival of even a freighter was something of an event. This preference was difficult to understand, for Adelaide, Melbourne, Brisbane, and particularly Sydney, were clean, handsome and lively cities. If they lacked the smiling, easygoing ambience of Perth, they made up for it in other ways. All of them had fine theatres, concert halls and art galleries; and for the less culturally minded there were night-clubs, fun-fairs, opulent cinemas and excellent restaurants.

Wherever we travelled on the coast of this infinitely varied country – it was possible to ski in the Snowy Mountains and go surfing on Bondi Beach the same day – there were days of swimming in golden bays and nights of riotous drinking with the chance of waking up with yet another girl in one's arms. The girls we met were usually white, but it wasn't always easy to tell just how white. Minto, for instance, was invited by a fair-complexioned flame of the moment to meet her grandmother, who turned out to be rather darker than the average Zulu.

My cabin mate and I had by then got into the habit of joining the younger deck-hands when they went ashore on the spree. This was inevitable in a small ship like ours where the cadets shared their gruelling labours, and, during storms the dangerous conditions under which they worked. The deck-hands were also more spontaneous and less constrained by the imposed values of rank and authority of the deck officers. The engineers were different, but apart from accompanying them to symphony concerts, the theatre and the occasional 'At Home' organized by local nurses for our benefit, we could not afford the expensive restaurants and other glossy establishments they were apt to patronize.

Meanwhile I had become aware of a growing restlessness in myself, and a disposition to question the orders of senior officers. I would reply to the bosun's sarcasm in kind. Flamboyant nights on the town with reckless, jovial seamen and playful girls seemed to allay this feeling, which was obscure in origin; but when dawn came round with the attendant headache caused by too much wine, it would return like an unanswered accusation. Perhaps in the last year I had absorbed more experience than I could comfortably assimilate. Or maybe the writing of verse accounted for it; or the intimations of other worlds realized, not only through sexual ecstasy, but from hearing great masterpieces of music in the concert halls of Sydney and Melbourne. But however difficult it was to define the cause of my discontent, it soon expressed itself very simply in practical terms. I had come to realize that Minto had been right about company policy. Cadets were grossly exploited, often given tasks to perform which the deck-hands might refuse. For instance, once we were cleaning out the holds after a cargo of grain. The temperature was around the hundred and twenty degrees Fahrenheit mark, and we did not so much breathe as gasp for air. The last job of all was to empty the bilges of the grain which had seeped through the boards and was now crawling with leprous-white maggots in noisome, putrefying sludge. The appalling stench cannot be described. Someone had to clamber down and try to get a foothold on that slithery, stinking corruption and scoop the stuff into lowered buckets. The choice was between Minto and me. I lost the toss of the coin, and most of my breakfast. There was something else: when I climbed in, several large rats scuttled out of their hiding-places and ran between my legs, dodging for cover.

As well as tasty jobs like that, cadets acted as night-watchmen, a twelve-hour stint but without overtime pay; and only cadets filled the water-tank above the bridge. And for all this, we were paid less than half the wages of an ordinary seaman. We were taught no navigation whatsoever by the officers; and only rarely were we allowed to 'shoot the sun' with the sextant at noon.

'It's always been like this,' explained the third mate. 'And we've all been through the system. It won't change.'

I thought that change was overdue, like the overtime the company refused to pay me, so I decided to settle the debt in my own way.

13

How Not to Retrieve an Anchor

My campaign of reprisals against the company began at Brisbane. There was no planning to speak of; I merely intended to flout the rules when it was convenient to do so, and it was fortuitous that Chippy Hollins suffered because of my first act of defiance. Who would have guessed the man would become emotional about a gangway? But if I had considered his misfortune at Gibraltar more carefully, I might have understood the chagrin he felt about his precious gangway. As for its romantic sequel, it has to be acknowledged that Chippy Hollins was not a lucky man.

The deck-hand who had sailed with Chippy on his first trip gave us the story. While Chippy was in charge of the windlass at Gibraltar, the mate had given the signal to lower the port anchor. It was dusk at the time, and what with the growing darkness, a rising wind, the rattle of the cable shooting up the spurling pipe with a fountain of dried mud from the chain locker, Chippy failed to notice at a critical point that the mate was now signalling him to apply the brake. When by dint of concerted shouts and hefty nudges from the bosun the message was finally conveyed, it was too late. The gathering momentum of the huge anchor and the heavy cable plummeting into the depths made it impossible for the brake to do anything but add to the din, which reached a climax when the chain shackle was wrenched with an almighty explosion from the floor of the deck locker. The whole shebang disappeared for ever into the drink, and with it Chippy's reputation for the rest of that trip.

To the tactless few who questioned him on the episode, he maintained his innocence with passion and eloquence. But no one was convinced, least of all our bosun, Dasher Daly. Dasher had an abiding distrust of graduates from polytechnic schools, but even he couldn't find fault with Chippy in the *Rembrandt* – apart from his tendency to lighten his labours with sea-shanties or a selection from *The Messiah*. But his duties at sea were slight, and it was not until we were crossing the Indian Ocean that an opportunity arose which called for his superior skills.

The mate had decided that our disreputable gangway was due for replacement. By then the ship's original colours had been restored: black hull and funnel, white superstructure and lifeboats, and buff-coloured masts, vents and derricks. The guns had been removed, and the bridge armour-plating which revealed timberwork that was varnished till it shone like new chestnuts. The brasswork was polished till it dazzled the eyes, and the ship's bell no longer sounded like a cheap tin tray. The ancient gangway was inconsistent with our new splendour, and Chippy was instructed to build a new one which would accord with the general effect. His prominent eyes lit up when he saw what was expected of him, and he set to work with diligence. Manuals and regulations were studied, and drawings prepared. In Australia he pestered the timber merchants and ship chandlers until he had procured the finest materials. The appearance of the smallest knot in a length of pine was enough for it to be ruthlessly rejected. At length the gangway took shape on number four hatch. Cleats were bolted to the stringers and stanchions inserted with new handlines were stretched through and finished with Turk's head knots. Finally the timbers were sanded and marine varnished, and the rest lovingly treated with dove-grey paint.

The finished article was a triumph for polytechnic education and Chippy was like a man who had reached full flower. He became obsessed with the thing. As he passed it on the way to more humdrum tasks, he would suddenly leap on the hatch and remove a speck of soot that had settled on its gleaming length. If anyone saw him perform these acts of love, he would look hurriedly at the sky and whistle softly to himself. Later we came to realize that not only was it his *magnum opus*, but that its hidden purpose was to indicate his technical superiority over the crew, and thereby exorcize the ghost of his mishap at Gibraltar. Maybe he surmised that if he could never retrieve the anchor and cable, he might at least salvage his reputation.

The crew regarded his infatuation in various ways. Wainwright, the second sparks, muttered 'hubris' once or twice rather forebodingly, while other critics observed that although the Board of Trade regulations may have been carried out to the letter, the gangway looked somewhat flimsy. The engineers were thoughtful. Chippy paid no heed to such ill-informed grumblings, and he ignored with disdain a rumour going the rounds that bets were being placed on the outcome of the gangway's first practical test; which added to the tension as we sailed up the Brisbane River and moored alongside a quay near the Storey Bridge. The lowering of the gangway was supervised by Chippy. He issued instructions in his clear tenor's voice, the handy-billy tackle was manipulated, and slowly the elegant contraption was eased down to the quayside with hardly a bump.

If the idling longshoremen were less than awe-struck by the spectacle, this didn't detract from Chippy's crowning moment, and he waited with apparent nonchalance as the port officials approached his master-work oblivious of the crucial step, so to speak, they were about to take.

We held our breath. Even the seagulls seemed to stop their squawking. But nothing happened: the mate welcomed the visitors and led them off to the captain while Australian currency changed hands among the crew.

The practical test was over. The gangway was functional as well as decorative, and soon it was being used as though it were just another gangway, although the deck-hands trod its length with exaggerated caution, especially when they knew Chippy was in the vicinity.

Now the rise and fall of the tide on the Pacific coast is huge, and a permanent watch was kept on the gangway to adjust its level in relation to the quayside. Since I was night-watchman again, the task fell to me after sundown, and every hour or so I would raise or lower Chippy's masterpiece by means of the handy-billy. For the duration of our stay at Brisbane all went smoothly and the gangway was never at risk; but on the night before we left for Melbourne things changed dramatically.

I had been ashore that afternoon and by chance met some of the crew returning from Surfers' Paradise. Exposure to the salty breakers had given the men powerful thirsts and they were heading for a hotel lounge popular with seamen. I had a couple of hours to kill before resuming duties, and the men were in good fettle after their day on the beach, so I joined them. The lounge was crowded, but we located two vacant tables which were quickly laden with delicious schooners of chilled beer. When these were dealt with, others speedily took their place. Talk became animated and the yarns started to flow. A feeling of good fellowship pervaded the room and seemed to swell out of the open windows to the wide world. The drinks kept coming round and the merriment grew infectious until others at adjacent tables were absorbed into the party. Two handsome girls, not yet on the blowsy side, edged their chairs closer and joined in the conversation. Outside, the roseate clouds of evening were melting into dusk. I lost all sense of time. I knew I should be on duty, but hazily I considered that this was a most agreeable way of showing dissatisfaction with company policy. Why couldn't it always be like this, I thought, with everyone laughing and enjoying themselves? Then I remembered the gangway and the extreme tidal rise and fall. I got up unsteadily and announced my departure. For some reason Jonesy and Waddington accompanied me to the door, and one of the girls came with them. Her eyes were the deepest shade of violet and utterly alluring. I kept my thoughts on the gangway and tried to make sense of what they were saying.

'They've got their gear wi' them, Jock. There'll be no trouble.'

'All you have to do is turn the old Nelson's eye. Savvy?'

I concentrated hard and said something like: 'It must be the beer, for I haven't heard a word you've said.' And I left them.

On board all was well. I hadn't been missed, and the gangway was intact. I lowered it a few feet, then went to the galley to make supper. At that moment the donkeyman came in with a bottle of Australian plonk, and an aperitif was deemed advisable, if only to take our minds off the anthropophobic mosquitoes.

After supper I made a check on the gangway, and this time paid out plenty of rope so that the wheeled foot could move freely along the quay. That would keep it safe for a longish spell, I thought, and hurried back to the galley, for a chill wind was blowing up the river. I made myself comfortable on the galley table and, with the remains of the plonk beside me, started reading the preface to Shaw's *Back to Methuselah*. The concept of evolution had become a recent interest, and I had been toying with great questions, such as: if man descended from apes, what will descend from man? If evolution meant a continuous refinement of forms, then something superior to ourselves must emerge in the future; and it was conceivable that man himself might have to take responsibility for the creation of this improved version, this *Obermensch*. For if he did not, he would revert or become extinct like other species which had failed to adapt to changing conditions, and nothing in nature stands still. Civilization, in the countries I had visited, seemed a very thin veneer; and already I had seen the glint of savagery behind the urbane masks, the jungle or desert waiting to swallow up the precarious cities. Our tenure of the world did not seem guaranteed. There was so much I needed to know about this important subject, to enable me to develop my clumsy insights; but there was nothing in the ship's library, and the Shaw which I found amongst the chief's books was the nearest I could get to it. For the first time in my life I experienced intellectual frustration.

Meanwhile it was late, and the effects of the beer and wine made reading an arduous business. At times I heard roisterers clambering up the gangway, and once I heard giggling as a party passed outside the galley. The giggle sounded familiar – it was definitely female; but I paid no attention and resumed the struggle of sorting out Lamarck's propositions from those of Darwin. It was an unequal struggle, the words kept blurring together until my eyes closed and the book slipped to the floor.

The river level dropped, flattened out, then inched up the quay wall; and the gangway, with no one on that sleeping ship to adjust its position, became inextricably wedged between the quay wall and the tumble-home of the hull. And no one heard the cracking and ruination of Chippy's finest effort, least of all myself.

Dasher Daly was first on the scene next morning. With a practised eye he observed the condition of the watchman and the destruction caused by the tidal river on the handiwork of a fledgling carpenter with a polytechnical education. Possibly he was grateful to me for my part in fulfilling his expectations.

For the remaining hours in port, the old gangway, which the bosun had thoughtfully stowed away in the 'tween deck in case of emergency, was brought into service again.

Chippy seemed even more broken up than his gangway and

his look of reproach pierced me to the soul, for his hopes of restoring a lost self-esteem were as distant as ever; but they vanished altogether when the man fell for one of our new passengers.

The night before we pulled into Melbourne, Mr Travis, the navigating officer, went aft at four bells to read the log and discovered a billowing set of feminine underwear attached to the log-line, drying in the offshore breeze. It puzzled him, and he mentioned his find at dinner. Second mates tend to be sleepy individuals, owing to their keeping the midnight watch, and Mr Travis was no exception. But the captain was more alert. 'I think it's time we had a ship's inspection, gentlemen,' he announced. 'Eight bells, tomorrow morning. And let's keep this to ourselves, shall we?' His fierce gaze travelled round the room, finally alighting on Minto and me.

We did our best to look guileless, but it was not our concern. Rumour had reached us that Jonesy and Waddington, after the first night, had passed the girls over to their mates, and thereafter the girls had been doing the rounds. Conditions down aft were Spartan and crowded, the atmosphere fetid and the cockroaches abundant. The girls must have had a pretty tough passage, and we had some sympathy for their coming encounter with the choleric Captain Davis. But before then there was a different kind of encounter for one of them, and we learnt of this from the cabin-boy next morning at smoko.

The cabin-boy had also made himself a hammock, which he slung at nights on the poop-deck above the taffrail. And that evening, as he swung under the stars, he was witness to the very oddest of shipboard romances. Apparently while the captain was making plans for the morrow, a dishevelled girl appeared on deck down aft to take in her washing and some badly needed fresh air. At once, by the light of the full moon, she saw Chippy leaning on the taffrail and staring at the wake with melancholy distaste. Her interest was aroused, for she guessed he must be a petty officer from amidships. 'Don't do it, cobber,' she said. 'Better times are comin'.'

Chippy looked round, and confirmed that the buzz of the galley was correct: there were indeed female stowaways on board. 'Y'see that bloody drink?' he said. 'Ah could just as well drop int't!'

'An' what good would that do?... Look at me!' she

challenged. 'D'you think I like piggin' it down there with them pommy drongos? D'you think I never feel like doin' myself in? ... But I wouldn't give 'em the satisfaction, mate. Anyhow, better times are comin'.' And with the reiteration of this hopeful remark she edged along the taffrail towards him.

'It was my friend that talked me into this caper. ... Of course I've had nothin' to do with them no-hopers below, fair dinkum. Not like her. ...'

Despite his gloom Chippy had felt drawn to this fellow victim of circumstances. He opened his heart to her, describing his promising early career and the small chance of its fulfilment at sea, before touching lightly on his innocence concerning the loss of an anchor at Gibraltar, among more recent tribulations. 'What ah'd really like to do, is leave the sea and start up a joinery business somewhere, then join the local choir.'

The girl approved of this plan and promised to make use of her contacts on his behalf when they reached Melbourne. Names were exchanged, they drew closer; and then it was Angela's turn to relate her story, which turned out to be even more heart-rending than Chippy's sad tale.

They clasped hands and talked late into the night, observed only by the descending moon and the cabin-boy with his head craning over the rails of the poop-deck.

Before the watch changed, Angela had collected her few belongings, most of which were attached to the log-line, then they wandered down the after-deck to Chippy's cabin, hand in hand. The cabin-boy, to keep sight of them, had twisted round in his hammock and capsized it, so that he spilled heavily on to the deck. The moonlit couple were so engrossed with each other that they heard nothing.

They were still engrossed when the inspection party surprised them next morning. The captain's roars could be heard down aft, and it was with difficulty that the carpenter was able to make himself heard.

'I say, Captain, sir. ... I'm right sorry for the bother I've caused to one and all, but I intend to marry Angela here, and I'll gladly pay her passage money to Melbourne. And we'd consider it an honour if you'd condescend to unite us in holy matrimony now we're on the high seas. ...'

This astonishing request deprived everyone of speech, for the ship was entering the Yarra Heads and there was land all around. Captain Davis was the first to recover. He decreed that the woman would be charged as a stowaway, and that Chippy would be logged for harbouring an illicit passenger.

Angela's friend was discovered in the arms of a trimmer, and as soon as the ship was tied up both girls were escorted ashore by a pair of brawny dock policemen. But they stepped jauntily enough down the old gangway and called out cheerful farewells to their several hosts who had come to see them off.

'G'd-day, you pommy bastards! See you around. . . .'

Before they were driven away one of the girls paused and glanced back till she had located Chippy standing moodily on the boat-deck. She gave him a curious sort of wave, more like a signal, then they were speeding off in the police car.

As for her fiancé, his desolation was profound. Once again his hopes of rebuilding self-esteem from the ruins of good intentions had proved illusory, and his cup of bitterness was full. The deck squad tended to avoid his eyes, as though misfortune might be contagious; but the bosun, now that his suspicions of the carpenter's general seaworthiness were confirmed, was prepared to be lenient, even going so far, once, as to ask the luckless man for a song. Chippy refused with a sombre but dignified silence which he maintained for the remainder of our stay at Melbourne.

The evening we left for Tasmania I was on the boat-deck trying to photograph a brace of black swans paddling up-river in dappled sunlight when I saw Chippy step briskly from his cabin carrying a bulky suitcase. I called to him that the ship was due to leave within the hour but he didn't pause, just gave me a genial wave and shouted something about having to make a phone call to Angela. She must have been the girl with the violet eyes, I guessed, last seen firmly attached to the Melbourne constabulary. Then he was hurrying down the gangway, and that was the last we saw of the singing carpenter. I wish I had taken a snapshot of him, for he looked positively blithe and undeterred by experience; he was about to have another throw of the dice. I hoped that some day his luck would change, and that one way or another he would retrieve that anchor and cable.

It was only then I fully realized my own culpability: if I hadn't slept on watch, or had prevented the girls from embarking, Chippy's gangway – and his pride – would still be intact, and he would have had no reason to jump ship. Our actions, then, were important, had an effect on the lives of others! I was alarmed. If there was such a thing as destiny, then I had been its unwitting instrument; but if there was not, my irresponsibility had crucially altered a man's career, for good or ill. I was awed by the implications of this.

14

The Governor's Ball

My campaign of defying company rules continued, but few of my early transgressions came to light, so no one recognized it for what it was. The mate knew I hadn't deliberately wrecked the gangway: it was an accident that might have happened to any watchman not permanently manning the hand-billy. I had been negligent, that was all. Other lapses in which I was unquestionably at fault were not so readily overlooked, but these came later, in Fiji and New Zealand. Until we arrived at those delectable islands, I was in a state of ambivalence, and I chafed that my rebellious acts went unnoticed, yet I was relieved that this was so. All the same, I was gradually becoming detached from the standards of conduct expected from cadet officers, even on tramp steamers. It was possible my subconscious was trying to tell me something that couldn't be revealed in verse.

We pulled out of Melbourne minus a ship's carpenter but with a general cargo which included a large shipment of sacramental wine. This was bound for the port of Burnie, Tasmania, though precious little of it reached the communion tables of Tasmanian churches. The wine was packed in small crates containing half-bottles, presumably for convenience of storage behind altars. As soon as the ship had docked, crew and stevedores alike found the packaging highly convenient,and crates of the claret-like beverage were quickly transported from the holds to a variety of hiding-places from which they would be uplifted when things had settled down for the day. They were to be found in clothes lockers, the mast tables, under coils of hawsers, and even dangling from lines inside the hold ventilators. The cook coming into the galley one morning found a crate of the stuff in the flour bunker. Breakfast was late that day.

In a very short while the SS *Rembrandt* took on a strange aspect, as though normal perspectives had slipped out of focus. It was rare for the crew to drink mere coffee from their mugs at smoko time, and smiling stevedores hummed dreamily to themselves as they worked the winches or stumbled about the holds vaguely attaching cargo to the trays. To maintain stocks, raids were carried out on the holds nightly usually by the men down aft, but the practice spread to amidships. Minto and I returned from a trip ashore to find Riley the fourth engineer playing 'The Bells of St Mary's' by rattling spoons on a range of opened bottles in which the levels of wine had been graded to produce a rough diatonic scale. We were invited to pull up a crate and join in the chorus.

Minto and I had lost all compunction about drinking stolen hooch a long time ago. We had filled the role of watchman, to say nothing of the water-tank, too often for that. The horror of cleaning out the bilges still lingered in the olfactory part of my memory. The company owed it to us.

Then it was our turn. At midnight, wearing soft shoes, we crept towards number two hatch, which lay under the captain's suite, prised open the tarpaulin and worked loose a hatch-board. I began the long descent of the ladder, Minto paying out a line of rope above my head, his own silhouetted against a triangle of starry sky. I reached the cargo and, by using a kind of braille system in that total blackness, tracked down a crate of the right size. I was lugging it across the uneven surface of bales and boxes when my free hand touched something warm in front of me. It was clothed and breathing heavily. Instantly I was petrified, but I guessed that whoever took the initiative had the advantage, though why I should want to disturb a drunken stevedore in that situation I shall never know.

I gripped him by the shoulder, shook him roughly and demanded to know what he meant by using our ship as a doss-house.

'It's all right, cobber. I'm on your side,' he whispered, evidently a man quick on the uptake. 'Just sleepin' it off, see?'

The bales creaked as though we were turning over, followed by sounds of deep breathing. I left him to it, found the bight of the rope and, putting a rolling hitch round the crate, called up to Minto to heave away. But I felt a slight unease about being aligned with a pilfering docker who drank himself into insensibility. It was different in our case, I reasoned: we were badly paid and overworked, and regarded the wine as payment in kind. The company wouldn't see it that way, but they were adequately insured against loss. So who would lose by it? Only the shareholders who would suffer a fractional drop in their quarterly dividends. But they would be comfortably off, likely enough, and would know nothing of the privations of a seaman's life which had made their dividends possible.

But a residual trace of puritanism prompted the reaction that my arguments were specious: theft was still theft. And there was no method of determining when a seaman had made good the deficiency in his wages by means of drink. Even if he knew when the balance was right, he was unlikely to stop there. I resolved that however I might break the rules in other respects, I would leave the cargo alone in future.

The less scrupulous members of the crew set sail from Burnie with deep regret, and rather earlier than the scheduled sailing date, owing to the rapid disappearance of the cargo. The stevedores, who had come to see us off, wore expressions of quiet misery, like mourners, for when would such an argosy come their way again, or one so poorly guarded?

The supervision had certainly been negligible, and the mate learnt nothing of our raids. So I got away with that one. Nor did he hear about Sheila when we were berthed at Mackay, Queensland.

It can be assumed that Sheila's English parents had christened their daughter before they decided to emigrate, since male Australians refer to all young women as 'Sheilas'. This must have caused her problems of identity in the years to come, and may have explained her preference for the company of seamen.

The port of Mackay consisted of a few ramshackle buildings and one milk bar, and was separated from the main town by two or three miles of scrub and swampland. At night the bullfrogs croaked unceasingly below shifting constellations of fireflies. A raised road connected the town from the port, and at weekends the girls of the town arrived by bus to inspect what the ocean had washed up for their amusement or to swim and sunbathe on the superb beach that began where the harbour stretched an arm into the sea.

This is how we met. The tide was receding and the tumult of giant breakers had lessened in force, when suddenly someone spotted the black fin of a marauding shark and gave the alarm. Without stopping to look round, the swimmers raced for the shore, Sheila and I arriving together, breathless and excited by our escape. We agreed that a milk-shake might steady the nerves, and went off to the milk bar, where we talked for hours, finally arranging to meet again.

In that torried climate our friendship quickly blossomed into a passion which we barely managed to control during the day on the beach. Yet for some reason we never wandered into the scrub or the vast area of the dunes where complete privacy was assured. Then, one night, after the last bus to town had rumbled past the café windows without waiting for her, she surprised me by saying she wanted to see my cabin. As I led her up the gangway, trying to master my eagerness, an old ditty surfaced: 'Once aboard the lugger and the girl is mine. . . .'

No one saw us. There was no need for a night-watch in a tiny port on the edge of a wilderness.

Minto was out on the town, and since the cabin was small and its resources limited, it wasn't long before we had wedged ourselves into my bunk, which was the lower one, and abandoned ourselves to a frenzy of voluptuous kissing. Darkness had overtaken the brief smouldering dusk, and I switched on the bulkhead bed-light, the better to admire her tanned, engaging face between kisses. And that's as far as we got; for Sheila revealed an unexpected coyness at the significant moment.

The humidity became almost unbearable, our hot embraces produced agonies of frustration, but still she resisted the fulfilment of desire for which every fibre in her lithe young body seemed to be crying out. In desperation I hunted under the pillow, which was now wringing with our sweat, and dragged out Dusty Miller's Palgrave, more to take my mind off my torments than in pursuit of good literature. The book fell open unerringly at Herrick's 'Counsel to Girls', and I quoted from it raptly, as though it were a sacred text:

> Gather ye rosebuds while ye may,
>   Old Time is still a-flying,
> And this same flower that smiles today
>   Tomorrow will be dying.

I learnt that a poem could succeed where nature had failed. As though a lock had turned, she was immediately aroused and the door was opened. It kept on opening for the rest of that feverish night until our bodies, crammed into that narrow bunk, were sticking together in a steamy, odorous lather.

Minto appeared at dawn. He paused at the coaming, gave an audible sniff, then ostentatiously making sure the ports were ajar, he stripped off and hoisted himself to the upper bunk and fell asleep.

There was less than an hour to go before we turned to. I had just time to smuggle Sheila ashore and have a shower before the bosun was on his rounds, bawling through the ports to get us out on deck.

That day's work was not unduly arduous, but I felt strangely exhausted at the end of it, and my knees had a tendency to tremble. At the time I couldn't account for it.

A few days later half a dozen of the hands, led my Minto as senior cadet, launched a lifeboat, ostensibly for a sail round the wide waters of the harbour. On no account were we to venture out to sea, the mate had instructed; but as soon as the red try-sail was hoisted to the truck and the sheets taken in, we were beating towards the harbour mouth as fast as the cumbersome craft and a beam wind would allow. Our goal was the Great Barrier Reef, but Minto and I were seldom invited to the chart-room and didn't know that it lay a hundred miles beyond the glittering horizon. We had hardly sailed a cable's length when the wind veered, and it took our combined efforts to maintain a tack of six points to the wind. The tide was running against us, so despite Minto's expert manoeuvring we were forced to return, watched by the supercilious bosun who had guessed our purpose.

At one point the heads had been tantalizingly close and the open sea was glimpsed, and I think all of us had the crazy urge to sail on and leave the rest to chance. I found myself quoting from Tennyson's 'Ulysses': 'To sail beyond the sunset, and the baths of all the western stars, until I die. It may be that the gulfs will wash us down: It may be we shall touch the Happy Isles. . . .'

Then the harbour wall obscured the ocean and we were wearing back to the davit falls in moods ranging from a sense of failure to outright depression.

The depression accompanied Minto and me into town that night, and when the third sparks suggested that we gatecrash the annual Governor's Ball, which happened to be in full swing just then, we agreed, recognizing a more achievable challenge. It was possible the town's more agreeable females might be there, maybe even Sheila.

Both surmises were misconceived. What was worse, the breezy candour and gusty humour that characterized most Australians were, on this one night of the year, nowhere in evidence. The scene that met our eyes, once we had talked our way past the reception committee, was a hall full of unnaturally posing individuals, standing or sitting in awkward attitudes, exchanging whispered insincerities and rigid smiles. They wore antiquated evening dress with all the ease and comfort of novitiate saints in hair shirts. The repertoire of the five-piece orchestra did not extend beyond the thirties; and the girls who condescended to dance with us seemed to be encased in their mothers' corsets, whether for reasons of fashion or protection we never found out. It was as if we were dancing with mobile trees, and I understood how a soldier in Malcolm's army felt as they marched to Dunsinane.

Conversation was equally unyielding, more like weight-lifting.

'D'you reckon the royal family are at Sandringham or Balmoral, this time of year?' one girl asked with self-conscious propriety.

'I'm afraid I know as much about their whereabouts as they know of mine,' I said.

Her slight form stiffened beneath her carapace. From then on we shuffled maladroitly round the floor in silence to the strains of 'Alexander's Ragtime Band'.

Just as my depression was threatening to return, the fourth engineer's cracked brogue echoed across the hall: 'Tell me, now,' he asked his partner, 'is the Governor a descendant of convicts like the rest of you?'

If the viceregal party at the head of the room heard this disingenuous remark they paid no heed, but some of the officials were getting restless. Nobody had ever barged into the Governor's Ball before and they weren't sure how to handle the situation. The Governor himself didn't appear to be bothered. Throughout the evening he had sat pink and formal, chatting amiably to those around him and occasionally getting up to trundle one of the womenfolk round the floor to show he was enjoying himself. Then a deputation, who were clearly not enjoying themselves at all, approached the great man, no doubt to disclaim responsibility for our existence. They looked like sheep-farmers or cattlemen from the Outback stations, hard men to deal with when not wearing tuxedos, but their indignation was making them human again. It was time to leave.

The captain was informed of the affair the following morning and we were confined to the port for the rest of our stay.

15

'The Land Where Corals Lie'

There are some days that live in the mind almost in their entirety, days that seem to be lit from within and return unbidden when life is not at its brightest. There was one such day not long after the night of the Governor's Ball at Mackay. Along with the other culprits, I was not supposed to enter the town again, lest we got up to further mischief, but there was no proscription on swimming. That morning, after a large breakfast, I donned trunks and sand-shoes and was about to leave for the beach when Dave, a young ordinary seaman, trotted up with the wholly unwelcome news that the mate wanted the water-tank pumped up.

I had acquired a few oaths by then and I let the man have the lot, winding up with the counter-proposal that the so-and-so Mr Gregan could fill the so-and-so tank himself and jump into it afterwards, for all I cared. And I was off down the gangway without so much as a backward glance and heading for the beach, where I hoped to meet Sheila. She was not on the telephone, so most of our meetings were casually arranged. 'I'll catch you up!' I heard Dave call out. I guessed he would explain to the mate that he had been unable to find me.

After a leisurely swim I lay on the warm sands idly watching the ocean when Dave appeared, clad like myself in swimming-trunks. There was no need for a towel in that heat.

'I bet you didn't give Gregan my message,' I said.

'Would you have done?' he replied, and dashed into the waves.

Half an hour went by, and a few townsfolk came into view carrying picnic baskets. Sheila was not amongst them.

'This place is getting crowded,' I said, there being about a dozen people scattered around. 'Let's go for a stroll.'

It started as simply as that. We set out along the yellow strand that stretched emptily northwards into infinity between crumbling ocean breakers on one side and sloping dunes on the other, interspersed with thornbush and what the locals called 'bunger trees', the fruit of which, apparently, were a wonderful antidote to dysentery. The sky was of a purest blue and the heat of the morning was tempered by a soft breeze from the sea. It seemed as though we could pad along in that sublime ambience for ever. There was not the least trace of man anywhere except for a lone white sail far out to sea, and only an occasional coconut husk or fragment of coral marred the immaculate strand. The sailing-ship intrigued us, and to get a better view we clambered up a dune, thinking it might be the *Pamir*, a four-masted barque we had seen sail under Sydney Harbour Bridge, or her sister ship the *Palmyra*, also trading in southern waters.

There are few lovelier sights on earth than a square-rigged ship under a full spread of canvas hugging the wind; and despite his understanding of the hellish lives led by the crew who man them, no true seaman can view the spectacle without emotion. From the crest of the dunes the sail was too distant to identify, and we sat there for a spell to catch our breath. It was only then we were aware that instead of being on top of a dune we were on the edge of a vast area of erosion, a baking sea of sand reaching inland towards a strange burst of dim forest. What was that dull green band separating sky from desert?

Of course we knew, and we stood there uncertainly for a moment as the heat pulsed up through our sand-shoes. Then, without a word, we turned our backs on the sea, that sprawling tyrant whose moods had invaded our dreams and taken possession of our souls, so that ashore we walked in time to its rocking beat, and slept in the memory of its seductive motion. Here was a chance of temporary escape from its domination, and we pressed on, without food or water, or even a hat to shield us from the sun, to that promise of coolness shimmering in the distant haze.

For mile after mile we trudged across that arid plain where nothing grew except in shallow folds of the sand where there were sparse clumps of a plant with tiny serrated leaves which folded up if their tips were touched, however, lightly. A few

monstrous ants stumbled around going nowhere. At intervals
the whitened bones of a steer jutted from the sand, the raised
horn minatory and the dark eye-socket seeming like a warning
from the land of the dead.

All at once the erosion belt came to an end, shelving steeply,
and we were tumbling down to the natural contours of the land
and more or less thrown headlong into the Bush.

The Bush! No term could so inadequately describe the noble
forest that soared two hundred feet above our heads and
beckoned us into its columned vistas of shadowy greens and
golds. As though in welcome, a cloud of sky-blue butterflies
enveloped us and accompanied our first hesitant steps into that
magical place, before swarming off between the sunbeam-
lanced trees.

As in a dream we followed its winding course into the forest
depths, pausing now and then to watch tree-frogs climb
prehensilely up the jade and silver trunks of the eucalyptus
trees, or parakeets threading their branches with flashes of
snowy brilliance; or to listen to unseen songbirds fluting perfect
calls to each other in a cathedral-like stillness. There was little
undergrowth, the trees were widely spaced between a soft
carpet of leaves, and soon we had left the desert far behind, its
yellow slopes concealed by a curtain of forest. Our only means
of estimating direction was the faint iridescence of the sun's
light flickering through the vaulted canopies high above. After a
mile or so we were utterly lost but we felt no panic, for we
guessed that nothing harmful could exist there; we were in a
sacred place, an Eden without a serpent.

Suddenly there was a drumming of hoofs, and a pure white
horse came charging through the trees. It veered on seeing us,
as startled as we were, then galloped off into the green distance
like an emanation from a mythical world or a medieval tapestry.
It wouldn't have surprised us if a spiralling horn had thrust out
from its forehead.

When the hoof-beats died away, the primeval silence surged
back more intensely than before; or maybe our senses had been
quickened by the encounter, for it was easy to believe that the
forest was a living presence acutely aware of our progress in its
midst, of every step we made.

Softly, like intruders, we padded on through that aromatic,
thrilling gloom without a thought in our heads but with an

unaccountable feeling of reverence and contentment. Now, I thought, here, at any rate, that hidden part of me should be satisfied; for I had never felt less at odds with the world or myself.

Far off a thin line of blueness pierced by the dark stems of trees appeared, and at length we came to a clearing in the Bush, a wide disc of pasture land as though nature had declared a breathing-space. It was about half a mile across and at its centre lay a swamp, the likely habitat of venomous snakes. We had heard bush-whackers tell of how professional snake-catchers performed their dangerous trade. The tail of the quarry was gripped tightly and with a sharp jerk the snake was cracked like a whip till its neck was broken. Such a trick would take practice, we thought, and decided to skirt the swamp, for instinctively we knew the clearing would have to be crossed. We quit the shade and, taking a bearing from the sun, headed for what we assumed to be the north side of the clearing. The heat came down like a lid on a frying-pan.

Then we saw the steers, about forty head of them, sheltering in the shade of the trees towards which we were heading, reddish brutes but peaceful and commonplace after the mystery of the Bush. Their existence was a disappointment. Domestic cattle had no business in Eden. It was an incongruity, almost an affront to the purity of the forest which had remained unchanged since before our ancestors walked upright. But there was no sign of a steading and, like the white horse, they may have been wild descendants of escaped stock brought out by early settlers.

As we discovered, they were certainly wild; but just then an emu broke cover and careered along the forest's edge like a thin grey spectre, its long legs blurred with speed. It was so splendidly unlike the sad, tattered specimens to be seen at zoos that long after it had merged again into the backdrop of the trees, we stood transfixed, hoping it would return.

We had just resumed our trek over the clearing when something prompted us to pay attention to the cattle. They had left the trees and were advancing towards us in ponderous deliberation. They did not look peaceful now. Some pawed the ground, others trotted forwards a few paces till the laggards had caught up, then they were all spread out and moving in line like a cavalry charge. The trot became a canter.

I was used to cattle at home, and I knew their moods. Friesian heifers on heat can be tricky beasts to handle, for instance. But I knew nothing of Australian steers, wild or otherwise, and I guessed the usual controlling techniques would not be effective here; and if they failed, there would be no opportunity of trying another method.

By then the pounding of staccato hoofs on the dry turf made the clearing sound like a drum, and their huge horns were swaying and tossing in the momentum of their charge. We could not outrun them. There was only one chance, and that was fraught with different hazards. With a shout to my companion to follow my steps, I raced into the swamp, leaping from one tuft of reeds to another as I had often done over peat-hags in Scottish hills. Half-way across I came to rest on a matted clump of reeds and looked back, first making sure there was nothing menacing lurking under my platform. Dave was tuft-hopping with precarious agility but reached my side safely. The steers had stopped at the swamp's reedy edge and were snorting and champing indecisively, but they came no further. Nor did they follow us round the swamp to intercept our mad scamper to the Bush, where their herd instinct would be confused in the maze of trees.

All the same, we plunged into the cool, luminous depths with fear more than relief, and didn't stop running until we were out of breath, grateful to be there, yet not knowing exactly where 'there' was. There are no landmarks in primitive forests. The sun was falling from the meridian: that much we had seen from the clearing. By taking an opposite tack from its supposed course down the sky, we reckoned we should eventually reach the coast, but we had no means of estimating how far this would be. We were tired and hungry, and the desire to curl up under a gum tree and sleep was overpowering but had to be resisted. Hours later a pale ribbon of sky showed again through the trees. This kept us going, and the fact that our Eden produced no fruit, not even an apple tree.

When the Bush ended abruptly and we tottered into fading daylight, we were confronted by dense banks of thorn-bush. But beyond this we glimpsed a river, shining like a last hope in a failing world. It was our only means of getting to the coast before nightfall; so by creeping commando fashion on our stomachs we were able to avoid the worst of the thorns, although our sunburnt hides were lacerated and bleeding before we had struggled through to the slow stream of kingfisher blue that meandered to the sea and safety. I never learnt the name of this life-saving river but I can still feel the fresh delights of its cool waters as we washed blood from our wounds and sweat from our faces, then waded downstream along its shallow sandy base.

At every bend a flight of unknown birds fluttered whitely at our approach, the thudding clap of their wings shattering the absolute stillness. Frilled lizards stuck out tongues at us, and weird fish dithered around our feet. There was one bird I did recognize: a glossy ibis which rose elegantly into the air, an epitome of beauty in motion, the graceful wing-beats and delicately arching neck lifting and falling with balletic precision as it flew lazily upstream, light spilling from its jet plumage in undulating cascades.

Our way lay downstream, and after an hour's wading there came a distant murmur, and a salty breeze sprang up, cooling our burnt faces. We were safe yet saddened, for we should never see that lovely river again; but the sound of our old enemy the sea was like irresistible music and we hurried towards it. Rounding the last bend of all, where the scrub and thorn-bush had succumbed to the encroaching dunes, we saw it at last and stopped on a sandbank to watch the river widen and merge with the glittering foam. Beyond the advancing breakers the sea lay placid and turquoise under a darkening sky pierced by early stars.

Then we saw something curious which we had overlooked in our haste to reach the sea. On adjacent sandbanks hundreds of tiny crabs had surfaced, their bright blue shells shaped like pagodas. Fascinated, we drew closer. The creatures had an extra pair of buttercup-yellow legs; and as we approached still nearer all the legs and claws dug furiously into the sand, causing their shells to spin round like tops until the entire colony was submerged, leaving a pattern of dimples to mark their where-abouts; then these too disappeared.

The sand had hardly closed over them when the sandbank we had just left sprouted a new crop of these peculiar crustaceans, which spiralled up with the same frenzy to reach the light as the adjacent colony had displayed in leaving it.

We had been under a blazing sun too long, and to make sure

we weren't hallucinating we returned to the first shoal; and the extraordinary performance was repeated. It was like a vertical game of hide-and-seek which the crabs seemed capable of playing for as long as we were there to provide the stimulus.

I should like to have brought one of them back to the ship for closer examination, but the experiences of that day had convinced me that Dave and I had been not only privileged but lucky. No venomous snakes or spiders had bitten us, which in that area might have been fatal. The charging cattle had not trampled us into the ground. We had been lost in an interminable forest, but uncannily our steps were led to an east-flowing river that was not snapping with crocodiles. Nature had revealed some of its wonders; and from the forest I had borrowed a sense of completeness and belonging that was unique in my life. It would have been sacrilege to destroy the least part of that world, so I left the crabs in peace.

The coastal trek back to the port drained the last of our strength, but eventually the harbour lights came into view, and the port buildings and the lighted window of the milk bar. There was a full moon and mosquitoes whined in the night air, a disconsolate sound. As we passed the milk bar the plaintive tones of an American crooner issued from a juke-box advising the customers of his lovelorn condition, and the bullfrogs seemed to be responding with eructative sympathy from a nearby swamp. It was a ridiculous postscript to such a day, and we were still laughing when we went aboard and raided the steward's pantry.

Minto had filled the water-tank.

16

Fiji

Sheila and half the town came to the port to see us off, or perhaps to make sure none of us stayed behind. We let go and churned into the harbour to a flurry of waving arms and shouted Australian farewells: 'Hooray, boys! See you again. . . . G'd on you, cobbers! . . .'

'I'll write to you, Jock!' called Sheila. 'Fair dinkum!'

Then we were coiling the heavy wet hawsers and wrestling with the diabolic wire-rope back springs and there was no more time for farewells, for we were off again, to somewhere strange and new where there might be other adventures, other testing experiences, and maybe other Sheilas.

We steamed north, hugging the Great Barrier Reef for a while, which emerged brokenly like gigantic green whales playing follow-my-leader, then pulled into Townsville, a humid but lovely port where gorgeous blooms cascaded down sheer cliffs above a turquoise bay, where cockatoos preened on every bar counter and the girls had grown weary of the local men. And thence to Cairns to load a cargo of sugar for Suva, capital of the Fiji Islands, along the seventeenth parallel of latitude. That trip was as close to a journey to the Happy Isles as we were likely to get, and our excitement increased day by day.

Suva was larger than I had expected, and more sedate than I might have wished, owing to New Zealand administration. Yet between the well-laid-out streets and colonial buildings it was still abundantly tropical, and exotic trees and shrubs bloomed exultantly wherever they could find space. Behind the town and along the coast stretched blue-green bush interspersed with native dwellings and coconut groves. By the shore a leisurely

Fijian trailed a chain of coconuts as he waded in the shallows towards town.

The quay was thronged with different racial types: shock-headed kanakas, tall and muscular melanic Fijians, who chatted as though everything was a huge joke; solemn Indian vendors selling paw-paws, passion fruit and guavas; an ancient barefoot Chinaman with a coolie hat, bearing a shoulder-yoke with panniers of ripe melons. An islander, lacking an arm and leg, came aboard to sell conches and cowrie shells, eager to show a letter from the mission man describing an attack on him by a shark. I bought two leopard cowries for a shilling, and I still have them.

In the town gardens royal palms soared above banks of oleanders, purple bougainvillaea and steel-tipped agaves. On shaven lawns small notices bore the inscription *sa tabu*, a curiously innocent use of a word with associations of voodoo and black magic. It seemed an impertinence for the authorities to enjoin the sons of heroic warriors to 'keep off the grass' and 'not to pick the flowers'. But, as we discovered, most of the Fijians had been tamed. In my grandfather's day they had eaten each other, and the last cannibal had died in Fiji just five years before our arrival. Yet the natives we met had retained their dignity and high spirits despite loss of sovereignty, and the introduction of paid labour and Christianity to their way of life.

Some of the cargo was bound for Lautoka on the north-west coast, and since stevedores were scarce there a crew of Fijians was hired and berthed in the 'tween decks. Work seemed a game to them and they tossed the heavy sacks of sugar to each other as though they were medicine balls, afterwards diving into the harbour for a vigorous swim, regardless of sharks, before settling down for the evening meal.

The meal over, the ceremony of kava-drinking began, with ritual hand-clapping and much raising of bowls. The stuff looked like milky tea and was made from a root which the women masticated before spitting the juice into hollowed-out tree-trunks. When it had fermented and was strained, it was ready for consumption. The result was a mild intoxicant, and though the authorities tried to ban it – more, it was thought, to encourage the sale of imported liquors than for reasons of hygiene – its use was widespread.

After the drinking session the islanders would bunk down in

the 'tween decks and sing Welsh hymns and Polynesian songs in glorious harmony. A beautiful sound with which to fall asleep, yet you could discern in that sonorous music an undertone of regret, maybe for a vanished freedom or an irretrievably lost innocence.

The man from the church mission disagreed: 'No, they're much happier under white man's rule,' he declared. 'Formerly they had the most blood-curdling practices. No war-canoe could be launched without sacrificial victims being tied to the launching poles, for instance. The dying man's screams, you see, were indispensable to the successful performance of the canoe in battle.' He shuddered delicately, but seemed pleased to relate other examples of their barbarism which the imposition of European values had mercifully suppressed: '. . . Whereas now, they have schools and hospitals, and of course the churches.' Which so far as he was concerned made the whole enterprise worthwhile.

He forbore to mention that Fijians could also enjoy the novelties of bars and brothels and gaols.

'And sooner or later we'll put a stop to kava-drinking,' he added. 'Or at least make it harmless and sanitary.'

This would mean that the islander would have to work for the white man to earn money to buy white man's booze. And if he squandered his wages on the unaccustomed intoxicants and got fighting drunk or neglected his family, he would be charged with breaking white man's laws and thrown into gaol. The drink, of course, was taxed, and the revenues subsidized the maintenance of the administration, the courts and the gaols, the hospitals and the schools, none of which had been needed prior to the European invasions.

The hospitals were undeniably useful, but mainly for the treatment of imported diseases. The schools too had a place in the system, by inculcating the standards of Western civilization. And if these proved too tortuous and confusing to the straightforward Polynesian mind, there was always the Church on hand to offer consolation for the trials of this life and certain bliss in the next – provided they had accommodated themselves to Christian resignation and humility. It all seemed a crude swindle on a gigantic scale, a self-perpetuating confidence trick; an insult added to the injury of their subjection. And the conquering races had come to believe their own mythologies,

their assumptions of cultural superiority, the divine righteous-
ness of their cause.

I had been reading H.G. Wells's *Outline of History* and formed
the perhaps shallow notion that since the discovery of the
Americas the Bible and the whip had become inseparable
companions. And I had read elsewhere that a Catholic bishop,
writing after the time of Cortez, had estimated that thirty million
Indians had died in the slave mines. But the Spaniards were
absolved from guilt for this because the slaves were 'not in a
state of grace'. There was even a sense that the conquistadores
were actually doing the Indians a favour by putting them out of
their unbaptized misery.

There was a horrible and peculiar insanity about all this that
kept me awake at nights. Few European countries had been as
rapacious and brutal as Spain when it came to stealing land from
coloured races; but the same underlying belief that somehow
the lives of heathens didn't count for much, seemed common to
all of them. And of course, for the Christian missionaries, it was
an evangelical imperative that they should save black souls from
perdition, whether the blacks wanted it or not.

I learnt something of Polynesian beliefs from a half-caste tally
clerk, a bright, humorous man who took coffee with us at
smoko. Apparently, before the white invasions, the islanders
knew perfectly well they were in a sort of paradise. Everyone
fished or hunted as they pleased according to tribal boundaries;
they ate fruit from the trees or drank kava as the mood took
them. Their only enemies were themselves, and war-parties
raided neighbouring islands more to express youthful energies
and toughen manhood than to enlarge territory. They had
music, elaborate art forms, and their government was run by
elders chosen for their wisdom and experience. There were no
class divisions or military castes, and they lived in surroundings
of superlative natural beauty. Life, therefore, was exceedingly
enjoyable, and they had no desire to leave it. There were not
many moral taboos, and no religious maniacs to ensure the
observance of the few they had: no Savanorolas or Loyolas, no
Calvins or Knoxes. And no implacable dogmas to make such
men necessary. What a world was theirs!

When death occurred and a person was extracted from this
pleasurable existence, the departed spirit had to be allowed to
return to it without delay. For this purpose funerals were

occasions of feasting and dancing, followed by general copula-
tion, ordinary relationships being temporarily suspended, so
providing the maximum opportunity for the recently departed
to re-enter this delightful world. Polynesian shamans were
reputed to be capable of seeing spirits hovering over these
orgies and queuing up, as it were, for admission into paradise
again.

What did it signify, the tally clerk hinted, if some cannibalism
or ritual killings took place? It was all in the family, and those
who perished would soon reappear in new guise, as good as
new; or, as we would say, recycled.

At first the islanders were reluctant to exchange their
reassuring creeds for the bleak Christian version of posthumous
life with its hideous punishments or unappetizing rewards. But
once the invaders were established, they were unable to resist
the alien religion, which taught mystifying concepts such as
'Blessed are the meek: for they shall inherit the earth'. How
could they make sense of this when it was the white man who
had disinherited them from their lands, and in which there had
been no poverty before he arrived? It was not remarkable that
the 'tween decks resounded with such pathos at night.

Strangely, the engineers took a different view of colonialism. I
had thought they were socialists, generally in favour of a system
of world government in which wealth and resources would be
uniformly distributed – 'from each according to his ability, to
each according to his need' – so terminating the fatal cycle of
slump-war-boom economics. I was mistaken. Their socialism
was essentially an insular English variety in which not too many
boats would be rocked. Meanwhile the Empire was sacrosanct.

'Of course we were right to grab the islands,' said the chief. 'If
we hadn't, the French or Dutch would have done, and the
natives would have been worse off.'

'And that goes for Australia, India and New Zealand?'

'Certainly. It was a race among European countries to seize as
much undeveloped land as possible to create favourable
markets.'

'Then colonialism has nothing to do with spreading the light
of Christian civilization?'

'Not in actual terms, no. Those things came later, inevitably.'

The chief was getting restless but I couldn't resist a dig at his
highly selective form of socialism, even if it prejudiced my

chances of an invitation to the evening gin session.

'But often enough you've protested at the exploitation of the workers. There's nobody quite so exploited as a dispossessed colonial native. Is he not a worker too?'

Purdie broke in at that: 'The Fijians don't appear to be exploited. Seems to me they have an enjoyable time of it under the present regime.'

This gave the chief time to change tack: 'And as for their supposed idyllic life before we came, don't you believe it. They were in the Dark Ages, their gods were brutal and ferocious, and their living conditions were fraught with diseases which modern medicine can now cure. Yaws, elephantiasis, leprosy.'

'True. It can also cure venereal diseases brought in by white sailors. It would spread rapidly here,' I mentioned, thinking of the carefree customs of the islanders. 'They wouldn't enjoy that.'

The chief exploded. 'Dammit, racial invasions have been going on since the beginning of time. It's an evolutionary necessity, and it's sentimental claptrap to think otherwise. You're naïve, son.'

'He's getting political, too,' commented Minto, always alert to my changes of interests, which tended to coincide with whatever I happened to be reading at the time. At the moment I was struggling with *Das Kapital*.

The quiet Wainwright then spoke, his cultured accents restoring calm to the tiffin period. 'It may be that the Polynesian, like the shark, has developed as far as he can possibly go. The Western invasions might stimulate him, might act as a spur to his latent powers and prevent him from reverting to primitivism. Now he may go forward, who knows?'

It was time to resume work and we broke up before this interesting point could be pursued. It was not an argument that would impress the islanders, but they were intelligent enough to know that their old way of life was doomed, and that if they didn't adapt to the changed conditions there would be no hope for them. The process would be difficult, if not traumatic. We had heard that the French were preparing to test the new kind of bombs in the Mururoa archipelago.

17

Stranded

Not far from a white and gold church looking like a puffed-up baroque meringue we found the tavern the tally clerk had recommended: colonial in style with a painted roof of corrugated iron, but the veranda was inviting and, inside, the atmosphere was cordial and relaxed. There was a view of the sea. The place attracted 'nice girls' we had been told, and those who were neither indigent nor affluent. It sounded right for us, and we were not disappointed. We got into the habit of dropping in after a swim or a stroll around the town. Our farewell party took place there on a night of some uncertainty concerning the ship's time of departure. The seamen I was with maintained we were due to leave at dawn, though there were contrary rumours on board. By an oversight nobody had bothered to consult the cook.

So there we were, downing the John Collins or the local beer and exchanging pleasantries with some local girls of mixed parentage while a flagrant sunset ran riot over the western sky. A heady fragrance of blossom was wafting through the open doors when Jonesy appeared, his short, round form dramatically silhouetted against the scarlet clouds. His news was brief: the ship would sail within the hour. All hands were ordered to turn to. We responded with knowing smiles.

It had to be a prank. We invited him to have a drink and meet the girls, if only he would stop this tomfoolery which was in the worst of taste. Jonesy simply repeated his message more urgently and hurried away.

I resumed chatting with two charming but dissimilar sisters and forgot all about Jonesy. One was dark of complexion with shapely red lips while her sister, though technically better looking, had a rather grey skin colour. It was likely that they had been sired by racially distinct fathers. They were both desirable, but I couldn't decide which of them I preferred. My companions were occupied with the sisters' friends, so there was no help to be had from them, particularly as a singsong was under way. The men exhausted their repertoire, and the girls replied with a group of lovely island songs which had us calling for more. Another round of drinks was ordered, and I had just made up my mind to settle for the grey-faced beauty, if she would have me, when Jonesy showed up again. 'This is your last chance, lads!' he shouted above the din, 'We cast off in ten minutes. If you don't leave now, you've had it!' He did an about-turn and vanished into the night.

The drinks were taking effect and not everyone heard him properly, but the company were in a mood of convivial immediacy, and any threat to its continuance was to be treated with disdain. 'Stop playing games, Jonesy!' they roared.

More drinks came round, and the girls sang a harmonized version of 'Isa Lei', an island song of farewell filled with a tender melancholy. The dark girl was the better singer, and I had almost decided to transfer my affections when Waddington muttered in my ear: 'I suppose there's no harm in goin' down to 'ave a look, like. . . . If she's still there, we can always come back.'

I doubted that, for it was late and the owner was looking pointedly at the clock. Besides which, our money was spent. If the *Rembrandt had* forsaken us, we had no place to go, unless the girls were prepared to offer the famous Polynesian hospitality, but that couldn't be taken for granted. Already some of the girls were saying good-night. I noted complacently that the sisters had made no move. Tomorrow could look after itself.

Later, what was left of the party wandered down to the harbour in a thoughtful mood, our high spirits having leaked away imperceptibly, leaving plenty of room for sudden well-founded doubts. Jonesy had not been playing games. The pier was deserted, and far out to sea the masthead lights of the SS *Rembrandt* heading westwards twinkled among the stars on the black horizon. It was a sobering predicament. Her quarters were uncomfortable, and she was a swine to steer in rough weather; but the old tub had been a sort of home, and now she was slipping out of our lives. Irrationally we felt hurt and betrayed. She had no business to behave like this: it was an unnatural act, like that of a mother abandoning her children.

We were cold standing there, but that was nothing compared with the chill sense of loneliness that set in when her lights were hidden by a distant headland. We were stranded and penniless.

'Bloody hell,' murmured Waddington. 'What do we do now?' At thirty, he was the oldest seaman there, but his experience had not prepared him for this situation.

Then came Clive and Spiers; young Dave, and a fellow Scot from St Andrews, Jack Shepheard, a fine baritone who always led the singing. He was not singing now. Finally, a couple of hands we had picked up in Sydney to replace deserters. Dusty Millar had jumped ship by then, and was rumoured to have gone bush-whacking in the Outback with some itinerant cane-cutters. He would have been useful here.

The sisters edged closer. 'If you like, Jock, we can put you up for the night. Not the others. Too many,' they said with genuine regret in their quiet voices. My heart leapt at this suggestion while my imagination seethed with scandalous possibilities.

'Come on, Jock,' said Spiers, who hadn't heard the girls' invitation. 'You're the officer here. Think of something.'

All I could think of was the intoxicating presence of the sisters at my side, and of how there was no longer a problem of choice. Two of their friends had come along, but they weren't obviously attached to anyone. Moreover, in terms of numbers, the girls were like the lifeboats of the *Titanic*: not enough of them to go round. I thought it was advisable that the men should not split up.

'We got out of that swamp at Mackay,' said young Dave. 'How do we get out of this?'

Dave voiced what was in all of their minds. They were rattled, and there was a plaintiveness about his question which I found hard to ignore, for it appealed to my vanity and a latent desire to prove myself. If Minto had been there, the dilemma would not have arisen. He would have taken charge, and I should have gone off with the obliging sisters. As things were, I never took leave of female company with more reluctance. They promised to look out for us in town next morning, then faded into the windy darkness, heading for the suburbs.

Our direction lay towards the town centre, for that was where

I imagined the civic lock-up would be located, our only chance of a bed for the night. A huge fuzzy-haired Fijian policeman on the beat took us to the place, and I introduced myself to the captain in charge, a tall affable New Zealander. I explained our plight. 'No problem, lads,' he said, having taken our measure. 'You can sleep in the constables' dorm. They won't mind.'

I protested with vehemence that we couldn't deprive his men of a night's sleep because of our imprudence. 'We would much rather sleep in the cells,' I said.

'Ah, but you haven't seen our cells,' he countered, and led the way to the dormitory. We remembered Beira and argued no further.

Not at all disgruntled, the kilted, barefoot constables yielded up their camp-beds, and, grinning broadly, they padded off to the cells. I hoped they slept as soundly as we did.

Next morning we were given a frugal breakfast and turned loose. I thanked the captain for his hospitality and outlined the next part of our difficulties. Somehow, without funds, we had to reach Lautoka, about a hundred and fifty miles by road across the island.

'There's a bus leaves every morning,' he said. 'Try the shipping agents. Maybe they'll sub you.'

His advice was sound, though when we had at length tracked down the company's agents, they were not easily convinced of our bona fides. I was made to sign several hastily composed letters covering them against loss before they would hand over a promissory note for the bus company. The agents would invoice the shipping company for the total amount, while we should no doubt be accountable to our captain. 'No doubt,' I echoed, trying not to think of that aspect of the business, and quite prepared to agree to anything, for the bus was due to leave. A few more nights in Suva and some of us might become beachcombers. The ship was short-handed.

At the bus station the manager shook his head at our document, never having seen one quite like it, and only the eloquence of the friendly tally clerk, whom we had met in the market, persuaded him to allow us to board the ramshackle vehicle which plied between the two ports.

We had hardly sat down when, with a grinding crash of ancient gears, the bus grumbled into action and weaved through the streets busy with islanders bringing fruit and

chickens into town. So began the long climb to the Nandrau
Plateau. The passengers were all Fijians, and in a jovial mood as
though on holiday. They were always like that.

I think we shared this mood for a while, for I remember
answering their animated queries about why we were travelling
to Lautoka. Naturally they thought the explanation was hil-
arious, and the news was relayed down the bus. Black, shining
faces turned to us with brilliant grins of approval, for it was just
as they would have behaved, and a spirit of camaraderie united
us that was nearly conspiratorial: as long as there were enough
people to flout convention, the law and regulation patterns of
conduct, life would continue to be the enjoyable business it was
meant to be. That seemed to sum up the attitude of the Fijians.

Fruit was passed down to us, and we sank teeth into the
pulpy richness of mangoes and passion-fruit, cloying but
nourishing fare. There was a long ride ahead of us before the
afternoon meal.

I must have fallen asleep during the inevitable singsong and
the sun was high when I came to. The wheezing bus had been
stopped to get its breath back, having reached the plateau.
Passengers were alighting, to stretch their legs or attend to
nature, or simply to admire the views of green highlands and
wooded valleys in all directions. There was peace all around
beyond description. Distantly the land sloped gently to the coast
and the bright sheen of the sea. Except for the winding road
which had led us from the town, there was no evidence that
man had ever set foot on the island. The world looked newly
made.

'If we ignored the bus and left the road, we could be
explorers,' I remarked to Clive who was nearby.

'Let's do that,' he replied, and without a word to the others,
we turned into the bush which ran along one side of the road,
glad of the shade but also eager to sustain the illusion that we
were lost travellers journeying into virgin territory.

We hadn't gone more than a furlong or so when the trees
thinned out and we found ourselves in a glade. And there
before our popping eyes was the model of every primitive
village we had ever seen in films or travel books. A dozen round
mud huts, each crowned with a cone of interwoven palm
leaves, were gathered in a loose circle round a clearing in which
skinny brown pigs roamed aimlessly and bantam-sized chickens

pecked at the earth. The place was deserted, but almost on
tiptoe we stole into the clearing. That's when we heard sounds
of movement and suppressed giggles. Bright eyes flashed from
dark doorways, which were no more than low, square holes
below overhanging eaves. We stood motionless, uncertain
about what to do next but unwilling to leave this scene of
primordial simplicity.

The invisible girls, encouraged by our immobility, appeared at
the doorways, their negroid faces beaming with mischief and
invitation, their supple arms beckoning us inside so as to
remove all lingering doubts. I glimpsed a dark, round breast.

Clive and I looked at each other questioningly, both thinking
of returning tribesmen armed with spears and clubs, and maybe
irascible after a poor day's hunting.

'The livestock are lean around here,' I whispered. 'They may
still keep a large cooking-pot for occasions like this. These old
traditions die hard.'

Clive too must have been glimpsing: 'Come on, Jock. . . . Let's
give it a try.'

But only our eyes travelled selectively round the circle of
bushy haired females squatting on their heels as though about
to spring. It would be like taking a step back in time, I thought.
Or like mating with one's Stone Age ancestors. . . .

We stood there irresolutely, on the brink of making some
genuine discoveries into the unknown, when a harsh metallic
braying noise shattered the silence. *Brapp . . . brapp . . . brapp. . . .*

The bus was impatient to set off for Lautoka. To have missed
the boat was unfortunate, but if we also missed the bus our
captain would assume we had gone native or become beachcombers.

In the depths of a British winter, while you are reading
Conrad or Somerset Maugham by a cosy fireside, such a change
of career might seem adventurous or even mildly glamorous.
But we had met beachcombers, seedy individuals for the most
part, who cadged drinks from sailors, money from remittance
men, and lived lives of precarious desperation. When they were
drunk they grew sentimental about the Old Country, or they
would curse the fate that had left them to rot in their island
paradise. It was not for us.

Brapp . . . Brapp. . . .

As for going native, Clive and I looked at the huts, the

clearing, the half-naked girls now gleefully converging on us, and fled through the bush to the road, then leapt aboard the bus. We were transported back to the twentieth century with only a few regrets.

There was one other stop, at a tiny settlement of immigrant Indians, where we had a meal so ferociously curried that it was impossible to distinguish one course from another. Soup, fish, chicken and meat all scorched the palate with equal intensity.

Sweat was still leaking from our every pore when we began the long descent to Lautoka, its promontories and islands already darkening against the sea's reflection of pale evening light.

'Maybe the ship's engines went on the blink again,' said Waddington, 'and we'll get there first!'

The problem didn't arise. The engines were in vigorous form, we learnt when we arrived. So was the captain's temper.

18

A Race for Life

Captain Davis lacked a sense of gratitude. Without money I had led half a dozen of his men across an unknown land back to the ship. Nevertheless, the men were logged ten pounds – this to be deducted from their final pay-off – but were otherwise free to go ashore; whereas I was confined to the ship, put on night-watch, obliged to fill the water-tank, and told bluntly that I would be reported to the company. Two can play the same game, I told myself, for I had plenty to report. Then I cancelled all thought of reprisals. What did it matter? The messages from my subconscious, released by the writing of verse, were becoming unmistakable. In the meantime, at the earliest chance, I should give them something worthwhile to report.

That chance came in New Zealand; but for the present, I eased the bonds of captivity by racing around the deserted town before dawn, savouring the last traces of the scented night as it bloomed into a painted sky, before returning for a swim in the harbour. These swims could be risky, and usually I waited till a cook or a hand was up on deck in case anything happened. From Aden to Queensland we had seen many sharks – hammer-heads, grey nurses, tiger sharks – and so far there had been few risks. Occasionally the galley-boy would heave a scrag-end of meat to one of the brutes. The shark would circle the morsel carefully before rolling over to expose two crescents of pointed teeth which closed over it with awesome finality. It was easy to imagine a human leg or arm disappear with the same unhurried efficiency. Yet these demonstrations rarely dissuaded us from swimming in potentially hazardous waters. Obviously we were lucky, but continuous luck can breed carelessness, can put you off-guard when an emergency happens.

Lautoka harbour provided such an emergency in the form of a lone shark of singularly regular habits which decided to alter its routine one day, and I still remember the taste of lonely terror when I think about it.

Many different species of fish cruised in and out of that wide tranquil harbour, most of them unknown to us. There was a school of one strange type, easily seen in the deep pellucid waters below the hull, which invaded my dreams and occupied them for years. They ranged in size from about six to nine feet long, were brown in colouring and had large, blunt heads. Riley, guessing widely, said they were manatees, which was unlikely; while Purdie thought they might be giant carp. But no one really knew. They did not look dangerous, but nothing would induce anyone to swim while they were in the harbour. Perhaps it was their numbers that deterred us. More likely it was because we knew nothing about them, their predatory techniques, their choices of diet.

With the solitary shark and its entourage of pilot fish, it was different, for we believed we knew a little about him, and our fear could be contained by his clockwork regularity. Every day at noon precisely, three pilot fish came through the harbour mouth, the oval-shaped suckers on the backs of their heads not then visible. Then, judging the coast to be clear, as it were, they somehow relayed this information to their master, and the huge torpedo form followed them in, a grey deadly shadow, the very emblem of menace.

The crew learnt to time their bathing to this unvarying schedule, leaving a wide interval before midday. It was noticeable too that dolphins romped about the harbour only in the mornings, which reassured us about the absence of sharks, for the two species never share the same waters.

One morning when I was still on deck, for reasons that escape me, and basking under awnings with a few of the hands, idly watching native sailing-craft drift lazily towards neighbouring islands, the cabin-boy joined us. He was hot and flustered from working in the pantry, and he announced to the company he was going for a swim even if he were logged for it. Did anyone else want to come?

It was pointed out that it was nearly six bells, that the shark would make its daily visit in an hour's time.

'We could have a race to the buoy and back. Quid stakes,' he offered, with an attempt at raising enthusiasm. 'It wouldn't take long,' he pleaded.

The buoy was about two hundred yards away. The pound wager was no incentive to me, since I couldn't go ashore to spend it, but we could easily swim a quarter of a mile in less than half an hour, and it was exceedingly hot even under the canvas.

We dived from the gunwhales together, but when we surfaced, instead of breaking into a racing crawl, for some intuitive reason, we kept up a steady breast-stroke side by side. And the words of a mariner's jingle went running through my mind: 'When in danger or in doubt, always keep a sharp look out.'

I had made sure there were no shoals of large fish about; but there hadn't been any dolphins either, and I began to get worried. So did the cabin-boy, and our pace slackened. We were about half-way to the buoy when sounds of a commotion from the ship came to us. Men were pointing to the harbour mouth and shouting meaningless words at us. We could guess what they were trying to convey, but was their warning genuine? Seamen are born pranksters; you could never be sure when they were serious.

'They're having us on, Jock,' gasped my companion, and struck out for the buoy with a brave show of indifference.

Then I saw it coming our way . . . and I shouted to alert him. It wasn't the shark but a sea-snake, about a fathom in length, with a grey and white chequered back and an evil head that glided sinuously over the surface towards us. We trod water helplessly and waited for something awful to happen. I knew that any reptile with a diced pattern was likely to be venomous, and the creature could swim faster than we could, so there was no point in making a dash for the ship and away from those relentless undulations.

It drew closer, and closer . . . then to our amazement, looking neither to right nor to left, it swam between us and headed for the ramped wall of the pier, where it slithered ashore and spiralled up the nearest telegraph-pole.

Only then were we aware of the hullabaloo on the *Rembrandt*. Men were bawling their heads off, some of them jumping up

and down, and all waving their arms wildly at us or pointing to
the harbour mouth. We saw the fin then and, fuelled by fear, we
raced for the Jacob's ladder, setting up twin wakes of foam like
speedboats. Now we understood the behaviour of the sea-
snake. Sharks are the most skilful predators in the world, but
they can't climb telegraph-poles.

'Bloody fools!' roared the bosun. He seemed quite upset, and
this surprised me. 'D'you want to get yourselves killed?'

Of course we didn't; but it was an interesting question. Young
seamen frequently took absurd risks, as though testing their
fate, and I was no exception. We felt indestructible, and to prove
it would perform reckless acts of bravado. By challenging
whatever inscrutable providence governs the lives of men, we
felt we were improving our temper to prepare ourselves for
the real tests to come.

An example of this happened in Melbourne, at midnight.
Crossing a bridge over the Yarra near the city centre, Spiers
declared he would pay five pounds to anyone game enough to
dive into the river. Immediately, a man called Ramson started
stripping to his underwear, oblivious of the traffic and passers-
by. Then he climbed on the parapet and launched himself
through about twenty feet of blackness and into the murky
waters with a clumsy splash. By that time Spiers wished he had
kept his mouth shut. But there was no harm done. Within a few
minutes Ramson was in our midst and shaking himself like a
spaniel, his only complaint being that he had lost a sock on the
way down.

That was fairly typical. Ramson was not desperate for money,
nor was he an expert swimmer. A challenge had been issued, he
had accepted it, and that's all there was to it. I had responded to
the cabin-boy's invitation to go for a swim in the same way.
Some day what we had learnt of the experiences might be of
use.

It was pointless to explain these things to the bosun. When
one look at that gnarled, mahogany-hard face, it was difficult to
imagine he had ever been young; but the second mate told us of
a wartime exploit of the bosun's that suggested he too may once
have tested himself against long odds as a youth. His ship had
been torpedoed in heavy seas. It was dusk and there was total
confusion. Some of the crew had lowered the lee lifeboats and
broke clear, unaware the bosun and the captain were uncon-

scious and still on board. The bosun recovered first; and no one knows how the feat was possible, but he rigged up a lifeboat to the radial-type davits – a survival of sailing-ships – and lowered the boat with the captain in it to the sea, and then single-handedly sailed her to a port. The captain's life was saved and the bosun was given a medal. He should also have been invited, for the sake of maritime history, to record his method of lowering the lifeboat. Normally it takes four trained men working rapidly for about quarter of an hour to perform this operation using radial davits. But the bosun was alone, there was a running sea, and the ship was going down. What the bosun had done should have been technically impossible, and we regarded him in a new light when the second mate had finished his tale.

I regretted the bitter arguments we had got into at various times, which owed their causes more, I think, to my general dislike of authority and his resentment of youth than to any apparent disagreement over points of seamanship or shipboard discipline. He deserved better than that. I can still see his powerful figure moving up the tilting decks in a slow charge, cap reversed and marlinspike at the ready, rasping out impeccable orders, goading the men into prompt action; totally fearless and infinitely resourceful. I never met another seaman like him, and I wish he could read these words now.

What old Dasher Daly might have said about the intimations from my subconscious can only be conjectured. Possibly he might have been less surprised than I was by the discovery that two distinct aspects of myself were in existence, in opposition to each other yet forced to work in tandem. Possibly he may have suspected it from the first.

In Lautoka something happened which seemed to hint that another aspect of the mind was present, a third layer of consciousness, deeper or higher than the others but in no way related to them. The heat was intense. Shepheard, Waddington and I were under the shelter of the boat-deck and panting for breath. Conversation had limped to a halt, and in a companionable mood we gazed incuriously through half-closed eyes at the blazing basin of light which was the ocean. Islands shimmered unreally on the horizon like a delicate mirage.

Suddenly I was aware that the light had intensified: the shadows cast by the bulwark and deck stanchions had become as black as tar; the matted, curly hair of Shepheard now crinkled dazzlingly, and the lumpy shoulder of Waddington was etched sharply against the luminous sea like a dark cliff against a lake of fire. An impenetrable silence enveloped us. Then, as though a moment had been plucked from the flow of ordinary time, the scene framed by the stanchions was subtly transmuted, leaving a replica of itself frozen on the air. . . . It was as if the pulse of the world had missed a beat. And in the strange interim I found that my mind was trembling with sensations of purest joy and serene contentment.

What had taken place in that split second? My perception of reality hadn't materially altered during that non-time; but all things within my field of vision, including the air that surrounded them, had briefly become charged with an uncanny significance that seemed to be on the verge of revealing an immense and delectable secret.

I shall never know how long I remained in this trance-like state. Maybe a gull or frigate bird floating across the sky broke the spell and eased me into the present. But where had I been before the spell was broken? And what had induced that mysterious sense of peace and happiness?

I thought of several explanations, all of them useless: that I had drifted into a daydream and my subconscious had invented the whole thing. That the drowsy heat and the glitter of the sea had hypnotized me. But I was convinced by the intensity of the experience that it had been no daydream. For the same reason, I rejected the possibility of hallucination. And everything in the scene had stayed in place, unchanged and motionless. Only their underlying *meaning* had changed. In that instant, something like a new dimension of the world, or a different version of reality, had disclosed its existence and evoked a response from yet another unsuspected part of my mind. My skull was more crowded than I thought.

Then Shepheard stirred and said something, and the ordinary world broke in. If anything unusual had occurred to the others, they didn't refer to it, and I was not inclined to introduce the subject. Metaphysics is not a topic much bandied about among merchant seamen.

19

The Long White Cloud

A serrated ridge with scree plunging a thousand feet on either side barred further progress. And where the ridge joined the massif, the snowy cone of Mount Egmont began its steep ascent, cutting crystal sharp into an intensely blue sky. A fine wind sang in our ears like the sustained vibrato of a violin's high note. The view all round was immense, and in a mood of elation we scrambled up a nearby knoll and dropped panting on its stony top to drink in the blue-green spaciousness of the scene.

The knoll was about a mile above sea-level and we had the sensation that we were sitting on top of the world. The mountain was sacred to the Maoris, but to Clive and me it had another kind of importance: if not the last place on earth, it was as far from our homelands as we would ever go. An axis through Dover would emerge a few hundred miles away. It was world's end, or at least one of the 'round earth's imagined corners', and a strange feeling of poignancy mingled with my geographical awe.

Clive lit a cigarette and with difficulty I got my new pipe going. We settled back, at peace with the universe. Below, outcrops of ferny rocks obscured the charabanc, which had brought us here, and the chalet where the others were having cooling drinks. It was a relief to get away from the crew once in a while. Clive and I had struck up a friendship over the poetry of Walter Scott, which he could quote by the page. At that moment I half expected him to recite something like

> Breathes there a man, with soul so dead,
> Who never to himself hath said,
>   This is my own, my native land!

Clive's quotations weren't always appropriate. Confronted by that stupendous view, however, he was silent.

Dense forest covered the skirts of the mountain, rolled over foothills and spread widely to gentler terrain where clearings marked the locations of steadings and pasture land, emerald green against the darker Bush country. Beyond lay undulating farmland and woods hazy in the sunlight. In the far distance the coast ribboned north to the Taranaki Bight, and westwards the sheen of the ocean swept up to the burnished horizon with its frieze of bulbous white clouds. From our height it was possible to see the curvature of the earth.

It was a time for reflection. For the moment we were detached from the scurry of life: it was down there, but out of sight. Like the solitary mountain on whose back we lay, we were isolated from the influence of worldly events. It was a time to make use of this isolation, to consider objectively the shape our lives would take. Thus far had we come. What of the future?

About forty miles away we could discern the broken volcanic tuffs jutting from the sea at New Plymouth where the *Rembrandt* was berthed. Soon the old ship would take the long trip home. A serious question was: would we be on board when she left? Several of the crew had jumped ship already, attracted by the beauty of the country, the blithe climate, the unruffled way of life. The population was sparse, and opportunities abounded for determined settlers. Potential farmland could be bought cheaply, virgin bush for next to nothing for those prepared to clear it. All that was needed was hard work and enough capital to survive the first lean years. It was a young country with little legislation, less tradition, and virtually no class system. There were few signs of Maori unrest or resentment: they did exist but were kept at a distance. In the future there might come a day of reckoning but, on the surface, relations between the races were superior to those in most colonial countries. White New Zealanders pointed out with justifiable pride that there were two Maori Members of Parliament. Others would follow.

We learnt of these tempting details while the ship was in Auckland at a time when the dockers were striking for the forty-hour week, which to seamen used to a fifty-six-hour week was an inducement in itself to remain in those lovely islands. The strike prolonged our stay there, and the closer acquaintance of the town this allowed, revealed the most persuasive allurement of all: there was a serious shortage of men. So every evening, what members of crew could get away, would take the ferry from our docking-place on the north shore and sail to the town across the superb natural harbour, which was usually enflamed by a fantastic sunset. Once ashore they would meet a variety of obliging females, some white, others Maori-coloured, and the rest of every imaginable shade in between. The apolitical power of love had already transcended racial prejudice to some extent, and in that lusty city it was conceivable that in the remote future ethnical differences might disappear altogether and be happily forgotten, with the creation of a new species of man, a true New Zealander.

Auckland then was an Arcadia for amorously inclined seamen, and it was remarkable that not more of them had jumped ship when we finally set sail for New Plymouth in Taranaki Territory. And from that quiet little port one could see the white pyramid of Mount Egmont rising above the distant wooded hills like an antipodean Fujiyama, a compelling thrust of volcanic rock that seemed to preside over the territory as though it were a living thing and aware of what went on beneath its lofty gaze.

Mountains had always fascinated me, and I longed to climb this one, which was twice the height of any in Scotland; but there didn't seem much hope of it till word got round that a charabanc tour had been organized by the Flying Angel Mission. Branches of this worthy body were to be found in most ports, and their avowed aims of providing alternative recreations, such as draughts and table-tennis, to the usual pursuits of seamen, were regarded with affectionate contempt. But with the prospect of this tour enthusiasm was aroused, even if it included a church service afterwards, which was the usual penalty for succumbing to Flying Angel entertainments.

The bus had stopped half-way up the mountain at a chalet-type restaurant. From that height the view was spectacular enough, but Clive and I had ventured further up the slopes until the obstacle of the ridge had diverted us to the knoll; and there we lay, smoking our tobacco, thinking of the future. . . .

Suddenly I seemed to have a bizarre vision. It was as though I could see the meandering course of our travels in a foreshortened perspective of time, and for an eerie moment I had the illusion that we were adjacent to the gods and shared their power to alter the direction of our lives: as though we could push counters of ourselves across the chequer-board of life at will; as though we were the purposive instruments of our own destiny.

'Will you jump ship?' asked Clive. The vision fled, but it was a reasonable question in the circumstances.

'Will you?'

'I'm not sure,' he said.

Since Clive came from Hull, I couldn't fathom his hesitation. He was a new type of seaman, one of those who hadn't so much responded to the call of the sea as resisted a call to arms, in the form of army conscription. A seaman by default.

'I'd like to get involved with big engineering works,' he said. 'Dams, bridges, that kind of thing. Something to show for your efforts. Something permanent. Not like the sea.'

I thought of rain falling in the English Midlands, the queues and ration books, the leaden authority of the bureaucrats. At the same time a melange of all the places we had seen since leaving Newport flitted through my mind. The journey back was twelve thousand miles. Who could tell what strange sights or adventures lay ahead? I touched on these things.

'But we're young, and it's all fresh and new,' he replied. 'Ultimately what satisfaction will you get from shunting cargo from one port to another? What'll you have to show for it at the end of your life except a parrot and some souvenirs?'

'"Rich eyes and poor hands,"' I quoted, picturing myself as an old sea-dog replete with experience, sitting in the best chair of a decent club, regaling younger members with tales of long ago and far away, of storms and mutinies and shipwrecks. But even as I fantasized, I was aware that Clive's words had reached a receptive area of my mind, and that their significance was overwhelming my imagined scene till the old sea-dog seemed like the club bore.

In the long term Clive could be right. A seaman's life, by definition, was transient and circumstantial. A day might come when one had seen it all, when variety would have lost the power to astonish and even the exotic became commonplace. And there was certainly something deeply appealing about leaving one's mark on the world, however small; an enduring statement of some kind to outlast the fleeting stuff of personal life. 'Oh yes,' acquaintances would say in later years, 'he painted that picture. . . .' Or wrote that book or designed that building; had provided more useful proof of his existence than a lump of marble with a hackneyed epitaph. That last rest might come more peacefully if one had added a more original testament than a headstone to the sum of human achievement.

With a start I realized I had been thinking of my own death as a tangible fact. This was new, and absurd. I was young and fit, the land of Cockaigne was at my feet, and soon the ship would carry me to other lands with their own share of wonders and excitements. The book of my life had barely opened, and I had skipped through to the last page in an attempt to guess how I should feel then. It was more than absurd, it was morbid, and some lines of Cardinal Newman's came to mind:

> . . . I do not ask to see
> The distant scene – one step, enough for me.

The sun was crawling down the sky above the all too viewable Pacific. It was time for us to make our way down to the chalet. Of course the charabanc had long since gone. Missing essential transport was becoming a habit of mine. Maybe my subversive *alter ego* was up to his mischievous tricks again.

20

Missing Persons

When we considered the prospect of a two days' march ahead, sleeping rough on the way, the god-like calm deserted us and we trudged down the twisting hill road feeling humanly vulnerable again. After a mile or so the view contracted as we dropped below the tree-line until the road was like the bed of a channel between the looming walls of the forest. The Bush was taller and more impenetrable than in Queensland, but at least we weren't lost. All we had to do was follow the road and there was bound to be a settlement of some kind along the way.

It was growing dark when the forest thinned out into hilly farm country, but still there were no lights of a town, nor had there been any passing traffic from which we could hitch a lift. Hours later the Bush closed in again.

'We're sure to come to a farm sooner or later,' said Clive. 'We'll ask them for a bunk-down in a barn.' Then he had a better idea: 'What about asking them for a job? The *Rembrandt* won't leave for a fortnight, and we can see something of the country.'

The sombre woods were not inviting and the night air was chill.

'Let's try for somewhere to sleep first, then we'll think about it. If we ever see a farm, that is. . . .'

But shortly afterwards, the lights of a house shone through trees not far from the road, and footsore and hungry we limped up the drive and knocked on the door. We explained the facts to the young farmer and his wife who, in some wonderment, had opened the door. Strangers were infrequent, particularly at night. But the couple were the soul of hospitality, a meal was provided, and after an hour's amiable but comatose conversation we were led off to the spare rooms.

We slept like dead men but woke next morning thoroughly refreshed and eager to pay for our board and lodging by helping out on odd jobs about the farm. A fragrance from the Bush filled the air.

'If you insist, boys,' said the farmer, 'but the farm's in its infancy. There's not a lot you can do except clear supple-jacks. After lunch I'll drive you over to my neighbours. They might take you on.' Clive had mentioned his plan to our hosts at breakfast.

And that is how we met the Walshaws. Fred was a wryly humorous, rangy Yorkshireman who had come out with his wife thirty years before. He was delighted to meet a man from Hull, and he laughed uproariously at our tale. 'I suppose you might as well be hanged for a sheep as a lamb,' he summed up, and led us into the trim house he had built with the help of neighbours. A spirit of co-operation prevailed there.

'A Canterbury sheep in this case,' smiled his wife, who set about making tea.

'Can't pay you much,' said Fred, 'but you're welcome to stay as long as you like, and we'll keep an eye on the local paper to find out when your ship's due to leave.'

So Clive and I became farmhands. The work was simple. In the mornings we herded cattle across a river with the aid of a collie. That done we would chop down some bramble which had become a curse to farmers in those parts. After a meal, Fred would crank up his old jalopy, as he called it, and drive us round the territory to see the sights or visit friends. The country reminded me in some ways of the Borders at home, but nowhere there had I seen ploughing on hillsides so steep that man and horse had difficulty in maintaining a footing. It was lush, fertile country, but it could be tamed only with the greatest effort.

At sundown we returned to the farm and rounded up the cattle. Tim, a waiflike child of nature who was the foster son of the Walshaws, did the milking, Clive and I sometimes lending an inexpert hand, which the Ayrshire cattle were quick to recognize. The milk was skimmed, Mrs Walshaw made butter from the cream, and the residue was fed to the pigs. It was the easiest farm life imaginable, and it may have explained why the local settlers were invariably unhurried and good-natured,

unlike the dour, Scrooge-like farmers I had worked for on
summer holidays.

In the evenings we sat round the fire and chatted till it was
time to go to bed. After a sound sleep we were up at dawn to
cross the sweet-smelling pastures with the cattle, the woods and
valleys green and sparkling, and beyond, the silvery heights of
Mount Egmont, a serene and reassuring presence soaring above
the encircling Bush.

After the long sea voyages, it was an idyllic interlude, a
soothing respite from the sounds of battering waves and
chuntering engines, the gulls howling dementedly in the wind.
I remembered lines from 'The Lotos-Eaters':

> We have had enough of motion,
> Weariness and wild alarm,
> Tossing on the tossing ocean. . . .

The hidden self that urged me to write pastoral verses was now,
presumably, in its element; yet curiously enough I never felt
impelled to write anything at all. I was content just to be there,
my senses quickened by all the natural odours and sounds, the
limpid beauty of the landscapes, my mind sharply aware of a
strange glowing rhythm that permeated this unspoilt country
like a breathing light.

Nowhere did I feel this sensation more intensely than in the
Bush. Fred and a neighbouring settler led us into its depths.
Unlike the Queensland Bush where there was little vegetation
underfoot, here the forest floor was covered with a riot of
creepers – supple-jacks – which grew in dense profusion,
snaked up the trees and criss-crossed between the giant boles,
so that you had to hack out every step of the way with billhooks.
Because of the slowness of progress the farmers had taken to
measuring distance travelled in the old unit of chains, a length
of sixty-six feet. In the space of half and hour we were told that
we had come barely four chains, but without the guidance of the
farmers Clive and I would have been hopelessly lost in that vast
green gloom. It was like fighting through sea-wrack on the
ocean's bed. But there were rewards. We located a rare Prince of
Wales fern; and from afar came the call of the mysterious tui
bird, a flutelike sound that stirred the heart and one paused
until it was repeated, swelling mellifluously through the maze

of interwoven branches like a tardy echo.

Then a more urgent sound was heard; faintly, at first, but rising to a crescendo as it approached, a ripping and crashing of something hurtling through the tangled undergrowth. . . .

'A Captain Cooker!' whispered Fred. 'Keep perfectly still!'

The noise reached a climax, and a wild boar shot across our line of vision a few yards ahead like a self-propelled, hairy cannon-ball, and with about as much destructive power against anything that stood in its way. Nothing could have diverted that fierce trajectory; a few more steps on our part, and limbs would have been broken. Probably the brute was not really in a hurry, and had simply gauged its momentum sufficiently to overcome the resistance of the undergrowth. That was how it got about.

When the awful racket had died away, Fred explained that to provide a source of food for settlers, Captain Cook had turned domestic goats and pigs loose in the islands and the descendants had become feralized; the boars covered with bristly hair had developed rudimentary tusks.

I thought of people, and wondered how many generations would pass before the progeny of, say, bishops or professors of fine art, forced to fend for themselves in the wilds, would similarly revert to primitivism. Suddenly our elaborate fabric of social values seemed a flimsy, jerry-built structure based on precarious assumptions. Maybe under the skin of the most civilized person lurked a Stone Age savage ready to shed philosophy, art and religion when living conditions deteriorated. Pigs are intelligent, but docile only when well fed.

A few days later we were treated to a closer experience of a Captain Cooker. A neighbour of the Walshaws had caught a wild boar which he intended to use for stud to improve the stock of pigs on his farm. Our assistance was required to enable him to 'ring' the animal's snout. The farm where the operation took place lay on a till plain between steep grassy banks. Six men were involved – Clive, myself and two others, each holding a leg, while Fred gripped the brute's struggling head as the farmer threaded red-hot copper wires into one nostril and out through the other. The ends were twisted together so that they resembled another horn. The hideous squeals of the unfortunate boar, piercingly amplified by the echoing banks, rang in my head for the remainder of our stay.

This was to be shorter than we had planned. In a recent copy of *The New Plymouth Daily News*, under the heading 'Missing Persons', Clive and I were alarmed to read a description of ourselves, our names properly spelt, and that of the freighter from which we had deserted, presently moored at New Plymouth. The article added the informative detail that 'the two men were last seen in Waitara' – a pleasant seaside town through which Fred had driven us one afternoon. The piece concluded with these ominous words: 'Anyone with information that may lead to their apprehension, please notify the local police station.'

Our intention had been to see the country and meet New Zealanders, not to be hunted like desperadoes by the police and wind up in gaol. And it was unthinkable that our kindly hosts should be charged with aiding and abetting illegal immigrants. It was time for us to take our leave. The same newspaper had given dates of shipping arrivals and departures. The SS *Rembrandt* was due out in two days' time.

Fred laughed in his deep-chested way: 'Nothing to worry about, lads. They'd put you in choky for a fortnight, then you'd be fully paid-up members of New Zealand society. We're short of good men round here. They'd give me a medal for helping to increase the population!'

We discussed it at supper that evening. It was pointed out to Clive that plenty of bridges and dams would be needed in New Zealand. But he said that he had responsibilities to his parents, and hopes of marrying a girl who might still be waiting for him in Hull. I had no such responsibilities. My parents would wish me to do what seemed best for myself. I was free to decide. There was no country in the world I would rather have exchanged for my own than New Zealand; but something made me hesitate, some faint intimation that there were tasks in store which could be performed only in those rainy northern islands from which I had been so glad to escape. In a clumsy fashion I tried to explain my feelings.

'"Breathes there the man, with soul so dead?"' suggested Clive, perhaps expressing the true reason for his reluctance to settle there. But the causes of my uncertainty were more obscure and could not be summarized in verse. I would have to find them out for myself, one step at a time.

We made our farewells to Mrs Walshaw and Tim, and the friends we had first stayed with; then Fred under cover of darkness drove us to New Plymouth. It was a silent trip. After many promises to keep in touch, and with his assurance that if ever we changed our minds he would act as guarantor, we shook hands and with mixed emotions made our way to the *Rembrandt*.

The lecture from the captain was noisy and vituperative. Clive was logged heavily for the trouble he had given the police, the shipping agents and, not least, Captain Davis himself. As for me, the report to the company he was writing about me was lengthening into a short story. He hoped the directors would find it amusing, but he had little doubt that, nevertheless, my indentures would be annulled. I was glad Clive had been sent from the room.

'I'm supposed to be *in loco parentis*. D'you realize that, you young jackanapes?' he roared. 'What sort of officer d'you think you'll be, the way you're going on?' And so forth.

'We've been away a long time, sir. We were in need of a holiday,' I said, unable to think of a better excuse, although it was true.

'Be careful what you say, sir,' he retorted. 'Unless your conduct improves, you'll have all the holiday you want when this trip is over!'

Somehow the threat seemed less than dire, and I got the impression that behind the Old Man's rage was an element of bluff, that he was secretly relieved that we had returned. Whether this was because he was spared from writing awkward entries in the log-book, or because the crew had been depleted by so many genuine desertions, I never found out. But the issue as a whole was becoming academic, for I had a few doubts of my own to resolve.

21

The Longest Trail

As the *Rembrandt* pulled into Sydney for the last time, the SS *Pamir* was tacking outward bound, her high-piled rigging animated and buoyant in the breezy sunlight. Yet there was something ghostlike about her, as though she were a visitant from the past. Not too far off, the new kinds of bombs were being tested, in the Australian desert and in the islands of the Pacific. The *Pamir*, and her sister ships, were graceful dinosaurs of the shipping world, doomed to limp ever further behind their commercial rivals until eventually they would be pensioned off, converted into training-ships, or they would founder in gales and a little glory would pass from the face of the earth.

The barque heeled in the wind as she rounded the heads bearing north, then she was gone. We shared the same destination, and she had a fortnight's start; but our old steamer would get to Vancouver before her. Not that any of us were in a hurry to engage in the race, if race it was.

The trip from Sydney to Vancouver is the longest a freighter is likely to make, almost a third of the world's circumference, and only the worst of cyclonic storms would force us to break the journey at one of the islands. Meanwhile, to distract us from brooding on the tedium to come, there was Sydney, which of all Australian cities was the most vibrant and bracing. At the first sight of the great harbour Bridge, like an arched gateway to a new world, the spirits rose. It could be dangerous but never dull. Around the city centre skyscrapers were beginning to appear, for Sydney faced the United States; but other American influences were less conspicuous. Gangsterism flourished, for instance, and lately gang bosses had taken to eliminating opposition by throwing bombs at their rivals, hence Sydney's nickname 'little Chicago'. There was no prohibition as such, but the bars closed at six o'clock, which was almost as bad for seamen newly released from work. The term 'rush-hour' had a peculiar emphasis in Sydney from five-thirty onwards, when the streets surged with a stampede of thirsty office workers hurling themselves at the bars, which were like machines for the efficient disposal of beer. Regular fleets of schooners were set up in readiness for the onslaught, to be emptied and refilled with impressive speed.

After the bars shut, for those with insufficiently slaked thirsts there were the sly-grog shops, often simply the front rooms of private houses where people sat drinking overpriced liquor in silence so as not to arouse suspicion among the neighbours. I didn't care for these places, likewise the cabarets of the King's Cross area where drinks were even more expensive and dubious female company was available. It was more prudent to visit a restaurant that served Australian wines; then afterwards to a concert or the theatre.

Occasionally, to meet girls and improve our foxtrots, some of us would go dancing on a harbour ferry-boat. There was also the bonus of seeing the Harbour at sunset which would still be swarming with yachts, their rigs inflated like coloured balloons, while lights began to wink round the creeks and promontories and the fading rose of the sky merged with the city's glow.

The ferry stopped at a landing-stage near the bridge on the north side, and if you were lucky on the dance floor, you could step with the girl through the illuminated jaws of Luna Park for an hour's pandemonium. It was cleaner than most funfairs, which I was still young enough to enjoy, and more inventive: the scenic railway was alarming even to seamen, but like the Crazy House there, it lived up to its name. On the apexes there were sudden vistas of tossing skyscrapers and volatile hills before the dreadful swoops to skidding ground-level, and then the great bridge was careering wildly into the sky.

It was a relief to totter from the carriage and seek quieter amusements. But after the hall of distorting mirrors, the disorientating house with no right angles, and the cakewalk where jets of air threw the skirts of the girls over their heads, I had had enough and was just about to leave when I was persuaded to indulge in a final novelty. It you threw a ball at a target it depressed a lever, by which a beautiful girl, perched on a stool connected to the mechanism, was plunged into a tank of cold water. Her discomfiture was the prize. My first ball struck the target and the girl, before she disappeared, darted such a look of hatred at me that I handed the other balls back to the barker. I had no taste for sadism, it seemed.

At weekends we visited the beaches, Bondi, Coogee, Manly and others, and each of them had its team of well-drilled, skull-capped lifeguards who from a distance looked like a squad of bald Greek gods. But their ability to handle lifeboats was not quite so impressive, and once we saw a team in formation attempt to launch their boat beam-on to the huge Pacific breakers. The result was chaos. The boat capsized, scattering lifeguards and swimmers, and causing panic to surfers poised on wave-crests. We raced to the sea, righted the boat and dragged it up the sands, then returned to assist the gasping lifeguards ashore. It was only a training exercise, no shark warnings had sounded, but the experience taught us that our skills could be of civilian use.

Bill the donkeyman reached that conclusion before we did. In time the ship was loaded, battened down and ready to cast off. Farewell parties had been held with friends, and they came to see the departure of what was left of the crew, for several more had jumped ship, the donkeyman amongst them. The night-watch stint would pass more slowly without his ebullient company.

'Let go for'ard! Let go aft! Let go back-springs....' The telegraph rang for 'slow ahead' and the ship was breasting into the roads, hull down on the longest trail of all. Then Harbour Bridge arching over the fanning wake dropped far astern, and we were homeward bound.

Our first stop was Vancouver, using Great Circle navigation, but the time it took us to get there seemed to have little in common with the ordinary divisions of days and weeks. Once more we had been extracted from the world of men, and we existed in a hiatus where reduced versions of ourselves performed shipboard functions like automata. The ship's bell governed our lives by measuring out the hours – on watch, off watch, mealtimes, all against the eternal background of still sky and moving sea. Sudden fierce storms would erupt the tranquillity, blotting out distinctions between night and day for a while; then it would be as before, a gleaming emptiness with only the chugging engines and waters lapping round the hull to mar the silence.

Sometimes large shoals of the blue whale would approach, and two or three of them would leap from the sea together, the largest easily a hundred feet in length. Nothing I ever saw in nature equalled those improbable feats of agility, and no one knew then that the opportunities for seeing them were running out, that those massive but sublime animals were doomed. They would accompany us for a few miles, then with fountains of spray gushing from their blow-holes, like an offhand farewell, they dived, invariably taking with them a part of my mind, down to the lightless depths where unknown monsters of frightful ugliness were reputed to dwell, the creatures of nightmare. Denizens of this kind were seldom discussed, but older seamen had no doubt of their existence. Sea serpents to them were facts, not legends, and their appearance was to be dreaded, for they presaged disaster.

The nearest to a sea serpent we saw was a weird cross between a barracuda and a moray eel, but with a serrated fin running the length of its back. It was caught by the galley-boy using a large butcher's hook, round which it had tied itself in knots in an attempt to escape, and the sharpest knife could not cut the brute free from the hook.

Other varieties of whale were sighted regularly, and many flying fish, but dolphins and sharks seemed to have deserted us, and most of the time the sea was undisturbed and the sky clear save for a lone albatross hanging motionless above the main masthead as though suspended from above. It stayed with us for days.

After an age we crossed the international date-line for the third time; and for the second time there was a week consisting of two Thursdays. Crossing widdershins previously we were deprived of a Saturday. 'Just our rotten luck,' the men grumbled as they chipped rust or daubed red lead that day for no wages. 'Luck has nothing to do with it,' commented the cynics. 'The company arranges it that way.'

Otherwise it was a non-event, a matter of chronology and geography, an item of information to fill a space in a letter home. We had no sense of having arrived anywhere, any more than we had when crossing the Equator.

The last mail issue at Sydney had been a mixed lot, which had the effect of adding to the turmoil of my thoughts just then. A girl I had met in Port Lincoln suggested that I should leave the sea and return there to work in her father's prosperous business. 'Sooner or later', she wrote, 'you'll get tired of the sea.' That I found hard to believe, and I wasn't convinced that business was my true metier. I think her name was Phyllis.

Marguerite's letter contained a similar proposal but with a different emphasis. From habit I opened out the pages expecting the usual flutter of yellow blossom, but there wasn't a single petal. A good sign, I thought, until I read these words: ' . . . and my father says, all you need to start a business in Athens is only four thousand pounds'. Only! And once again she hadn't taken my hints that there were severe difficulties in the way of our reunion. Now I should have to explain that four thousand pounds wasn't so much a difficulty as an impossibility. In lieu of Greek flora she enclosed another photograph of herself. I compared it with the first one she had given me at our parting in Piraeus. There was no doubt of it, she had put on weight; and forgetting other preoccupations, I thought hard about the future and wondered.

There was a letter from home. My father had retired, and they were worried about me. I had mentioned Marguerite to them, and they were alarmed at the prospect of a breach of promise suit. So far as I could remember, I had promised nothing but my dreams to the girl; but suddenly the adult world had intruded, a dry, sterile place littered with the debris of wrecked hopes and stale consolations. Or like a lawyer's office whose walls were lined with cautionary tales. What could adults recall of the ludicrous effects of moonlight on senses already drunk with the glamour of an ancient city, the scent of blossom and tentative sexuality? And how could their children sympathize with their practical anxieties? Parents and their young seemed to be doomed to mutual incomprehension. They touch at extremes; at superficial and profound levels. But the areas in between are as obscure as cloud-covered foreign countries.

It was a relief to open Sheila's letter, which also included a photograph. Her hair had been specially arranged for the occasion, and instead of the attractively tousled personality with a fatal fondness for the verse of Herrick, there was a stranger with four sausages balanced on her head gazing upwards with a wistful expression on her face. But at least she wasn't demanding awkward decisions.

The last letter of all was a sad one. My wartime foster father had died of tuberculosis. He was the best of men; and my letter of condolence to his grief-stricken widow must have triggered off hidden chains of thought and memory, for on look-out that night the lines of an elegiac sonnet formed themselves involuntarily in my mind, expressing my own grief. This was new. I discovered that poetry was not merely painting with words, or metric anecdotage, or rendering into stanzaic form imaginary experiences. It was an emotional force rising from within, with which one could articulate the rarest of feelings and give shape to ideas on the furthest edge of mind. Poetry could alleviate chagrin or loss, both for the writer and the reader. It could suggest the indefinable, and venture into areas where philosophy could not follow. It was the result of a special intensity of experience.

A gateway had been opened, and hesitantly I took a few first steps into a new world. I reread Palgrave from cover to cover and found that certain poems of Keats and Shelley gave me palpitations so that I could hardly breathe, caught as I was in a kind of luminous enchantment. Other poems written from this deeper level touched on fears and anxieties I had long since buried; and so the possibility occurred to me that I might actually be a poet. I was flattered yet dismayed, for it implied a responsibility for which I was not quite ready. If I should leave the sea my parents would be quick to point out that, as an alternative way of life, the writing of poetry was not a career: it arose from a condition of one's nature, and a regrettable one at that. Great Uncle William had suffered from the condition, but he had been a Church minister at Grantown-on-Spey and had never allowed his poetry to interfere with the composition of his sermons. I should need a more substantial reason for breaking my indentures – if I should leave the sea, and that wasn't certain.

Nevertheless, it was about this time that I began to think seriously of architecture, for interest in that subject had run like a descant through all my visits to foreign places: the temples and orders of antiquity in Greece, the mosques and minarets of Algeria and Egypt, the cathedrals of Mozambique, and even the modern style in the Australian cities. The art master at school had been contemptuous of my first choice of career. 'Idiot,' he had said. 'Travel broadens the mind, it doesn't deepen it.' One could argue about that, but I knew now what he meant. He had wanted me to go to art college, not the nautical variety.

Then I recalled a rainy afternoon at home when, bored with working out some problem of astronomical trigonometry, I had started sketching on my jotter an isometric projection of a cathedral from an octagonal plan. So ... there might be an architect inside of me as well. It was all very confusing. What should I do for the best? Greece and Marguerite, or South Australia and Phyllis? Pursue the precarious life of a writer, or become a farmer in Taranaki with the Walshaws? Or remain at sea and grow into a Mr Gregan or Captain Davis? But that was unthinkable. The Old Man hadn't been seen for days. What sort of life was that? The loneliness of command had no appeal for me if that was the price one had to pay. And now there was architecture to consider.

While these conflicting possibilities preoccupied my mind, the ship was passing through the Hawaiian archipelago and the unreal beauty of sugar-loaf mountains pierced the horizon like steep blue pyramids. The main island of Oahu loomed tantalizingly close on the port side, and the glittering town of Honolulu was distinctly visible. The saloon radio blared out swing music, a tacit reminder of who controlled the area. Skyscrapers and Benny Goodman had invaded Polynesia. From what we had learnt of the islands, there would be little resistance to the onslaught of Americanism, and an ancient culture would be subsumed into a welter of Coca-Cola, hot dogs and materialism. In glossy white hotels island girls wearing grass skirts and lei round their necks would dance the hula-hula before overfed tourists. Hawaii would become an extension of California.

The world was changing rapidly, and the war in the Pacific, for which our bombs had not been necessary, had accelerated the change. A few days later, when we were sitting in the saloon after dinner, the radio announced that Mahatma Ghandi had been assassinated, and the course of history lurched off in a new direction. The senior officers looked grimly at each other and took long pulls from their drinks as they considered the implications.

'This will mean independence for India,' growled the chief.

'It's the beginning of the end!' he said, and the others nodded in glum agreement. They were crestfallen, for their most cherished belief was threatened, was in danger of being exposed as an illusion. At a stroke the permanence of the British Empire could no longer be taken for granted. The sun could set on it after all. My seniors looked into a future where the map of the world did not blush quite so much, and they were appalled. 'The Yanks are coming, the Yanks are coming,' ran the words of a First World War song. That was out of date, for the Yanks had arrived. They were the top dogs now.

22

The New World

Since the Ice Ages first made wanderers of men, their migrations had taken initially a southerly, then a westerly route, following the sun in the belief that the life-giver would lead to countries of plenty, if not promised lands. So it seemed contrary to immemorial practice to approach America from the west, to steal up on its blind side, as it were, and take it by surprise. Instead it was a ghostly sign from the continent which took us by surprise.

Progress across the Pacific had been slow, barely nine knots. The old ship needed a rest, and the men were desperate to stamp their feet on firm ground and meet people who resembled their shipmates as little as possible, for, once more, a localized misanthropy had settled on the crew like an epidemic. Latent enmities flared up on the slightest pretext and the best of friends fell out over trifles. Communication was pared to essentials and conveyed with the briefest of grunts.

Then one evening the azure blandness of the eastern sky was pierced by a dazzlingly white triangle. It was like a prismatic moon except that it faded with nightfall, leaving us gaping after it incredulously, our mutual irritations forgotten. Several peculiar phenomena had been sighted on that crossing: the delicate arch of a silver rainbow cast by a full moon after rainfall; a continuous shower of falling meteors which was like a sky-wide pyrotechnic display. And one night the entire heavens were illuminated by a vivid green light lasting nearly a minute. But no one had seen anything like this freak of the skies before. The aurora australis was ordinary stuff by comparison. 'It must be a mirage,' said the bosun.

His theory raised our hopes. If he was right, the thing was a meteorological reflection of an object concealed below the horizon – a snow-clad peak, for instance, like Mount Egmont, only higher. But whatever it was, it had to be connected with land. The thought of land made our bones ache with longing.

Charts were studied but with no convincing results, which, given the whimsical practice of navigation and helmsmanship on the *Rembrandt*, surprised nobody. The white triangle may have emanated from any one of a number of high peaks, from Mount Olympus in Oregon to Mount Rainier. But the nearest range was four hundred miles away and, because of the earth's curvature, it would be impossible to have seen a mountain as high as Everest over that distance.

The next day there was no sign of a cone-shaped moon and the mood of the crew reverted to a sullen aloofness. There was a brief respite when the forbidding wall of the coastal range came into view the following afternoon; then as we veered northwards a sluggish mist came seeping over the sea, obscuring the land and enveloping the ship in a cold, clammy embrace. Smoke from the funnel writhed about the decks like a frantic apparition, adding an acrid flavour to the faint wet smell of this country of detachable mountain peaks. The mist was not dense, visibility being about seventy yards. As we neared Vancouver Island, I was leaning on the deck-rail, staring into gray nothingness and wondering if I might be a phantom cadet on a ghost ship doomed to sail eternally to nowhere, when a large turtle appeared, doing a sort of side-stroke so as to keep an eye on our ship.

Now I don't expect many will believe what happened next; and it is well-known the mind can play tricks in fog and mist. But it is the sober truth that, as we drew level with each other, a sudden impulse made me raise my arm and wave a salute, as from one fellow mortal to another whose paths had crossed in a cheerless world. There was a second's pause, as though my intentions were being considered, then slowly a flipper emerged, and the turtle deliberately and unmistakably waved back.

I stared after its wake, feeling heartened and somehow humanized by the encounter, long after the amiable chelonian had vanished into the mist.

The mist lifted as we rounded Vancouver Island and sailed

into Queen Charlotte Strait, which led to the long fiordlike harbour of Vancouver. The approach to the city was spectacular: on either side steep pine-clad slopes, and spanning between a lofty suspension bridge of weblike delicacy whose graceful lines subtly complemented the rugged landscape. And dominating the area was the twin-peaked bulk of Lions Mountain, the start of an icy cordillera which terminated in Alaska.

Passing under the bridge we entered the harbour where ferry-boats like miniature *Queen Marys* plied to and fro. An Indian reservation occupied part of the north shore, and nearby the writer Malcolm Lowry was reputed to be living in dire poverty. Beside the reservation the suburbs of the town crept relentlessly up the hill in serried rows, as strictly co-ordinated as a regiment of troops on parade. It produced an incongruous effect in that wild terrain. Some planner had blundered again. It was rare, in cities of the new countries we had seen, for them to get the balance right between social needs and the natural environment. Yet this had been achieved consummately by the bridge-builders of Sydney and Vancouver; and it seemed paradoxical that engineers, who are not artists, could design aesthetic constructions that harmonized with their surroundings, while architects, trained in the oldest of art forms, could contrive nothing better than a grid pattern of regimented housing units.

As I thought of these things, it occurred to me that many of my forbears had been engineers; and another possibility was added to my list of post-nautical careers, for by now I was sure that a lifetime spent at sea would be too long for me. The subconscious messages had finally surfaced.

A week after our arrival the *Pamir* limped into port, her sails torn and bedraggled, the strakes of her hull blistered and patchy. All the cooks promptly deserted, and others of the crew soon followed their lead. The ship was a mess. What had been the pride of the seas was now a miserable vestige of her former glory, a pathetic broken-winged anachronism that risked the lives of its crew for the sake of a romantic ideal upheld by the owners from the safe distance of a company boardroom. She could never have weathered the hurricane that helped us along our homeward course two months later.

The city skyscrapers of Vancouver were similar to those of Sydney, but they looked gawky and unsophisticated, which

may have been due to the inexperience of the architects. It was a
very young town. Exactly sixty years had elapsed since it was
known as Granville, a rough-and-ready frontier settlement and
haunt of bootleggers. It gave an extra dimension to my sense of
time when I realized that Vancouver wasn't on the map when
my grandfather was a lad.

The civic authorities celebrated the town's birthday by
holding gymkhanas and open-air concerts in Stanley Park, an
area of great natural beauty wooded with sequoia and maple. In
a central clearing there were baleful totem-poles transplanted
from the reservations; but I never saw an Indian there. Perhaps
they believed their tribal gods had lost potency with the
displacement, or had deserted them after defeat by the white
man. In which case the totem-poles would be drained of
purpose, were merely ornamented tree-trunks for tourists to
photograph. Skyscrapers were the victors' totem-poles, and
year by year they would grow taller, possibly more elegant; but
Indians would still not be welcome.

Field-Marshal-Viscount (later Earl) Alexander of Tunis, then
Governor-General of Canada, was invited to the festivities and
to visit selected parts of the city. For some reason, the docks
were included in his itinerary, and one afternoon the governor-
general and his entourage were seen trooping along the quay
towards a white and gleaming cargo passenger. Our stokehold
gang had just come off watch and were swilling themselves with
buckets of water. A few Red Indians, who had been signed on to
trim 'tween deck coal, were likewise employed. The deck down
aft was a seething filthy mess of coal-dust and soap-suds.
'There's Alexander!' shouted a fireman, naked and streaked
with grime. 'Let's give him a cheer, boys!'

The suggestion may have been ironical, but the men had got
through a heavy day, and this was a break from routine.

'Hurrah!' they cried with equivocal sarcasm, and some of
them twirled their unspeakable sweat-rags high in the air.

The governor-general, in full regalia, turned to acknowledge
this spontaneous acclamation, evidently pleased. He conferred
with his party, and for a moment it seemed he might persuade
them to change course and visit the travel-stained *Rembrandt*.
But the officials had sharper eyes than the hero of the Western
desert, and they saw that the dirty British freighter had no
officer on deck to receive them, only naked firemen and morose

Indians who had finished their ablutions and were now staring into space with characteristic immobility. I was amidships but not wearing uniform, so I didn't matter very much either.

As the governor-general was gently but firmly led off to the smart cruiser where a tidier welcome awaited him, he glanced apologetically over his shoulder and waved a regretful arm in farewell, reminding me of the turtle and how it too was borne away by a prevailing current.

It is probable that the firemen were not being sarcastic at all, and were genuinely pleased to recognize a famous countryman; but their code permitted them to express their admiration only in disguised form. Displays of feeling generally were not encouraged, for that might indicate weakness of character, which, like lack of stamina, could at crucial moments affect the safety of the ship, and that above all else was paramount.

At Vancouver, however, our last major port of call before the homeward trip, the crew relaxed their rigid standards and talked emotively about their home life, and discussed the presents they had bought for their sweethearts and families. Even the grizzled old cook, whom no one could imagine having the slightest connection with domesticity, referred frequently to plans he had made to celebrate the reunion with his grown-up family: visits to Birkenhead pier, the music-halls, the cinemas, and his working men's club where you could get a decent pint of English bitter. A gratuitous warmth crept into his normally gutteral accents as he dwelt on these anticipated delights.

An abnormal virtuousness was also apparent, and the Vancouver police had an easy time of it. Drunkenness was unknown, fights unthinkable. The local brothel, whose red light glowed within sight of the *Rembrandt*, was shunned by all hands. The treatment period for disease might overlap with home leave, and that would never do, for discovery would mean social ostracism. It was as though the crew were morally sprucing themselves up for the coming meeting with loved ones. There were even a few who tried to give the impression that this was their habitual conduct, and instead of roistering round the bars and speakeasies on the look-out for good-time girls, they sought out more discreet amusements. They attended concerts at Stanley Park, where the comedian Eddie Cantor was performing; and barn dances patronized by office workers who dressed up as cowboys and lumberjacks for the occasion. And there was a downtown cinema that interposed between the main films a vaudeville show featuring the tallest striptease artiste in the world. But not even the complete exposure of this prodigy, which of course took some time to effect, could distract the men from their newly acquired moral rectitude. Maybe the sheer novelty of temperance and celibacy appealed to them, as a sort of challenge. But it was doubtful if it could last. The ship would have to dock for coal sooner or later, and that would be the testing time.

Our ship had transported bales of wool and hogsheads of wine from Australia; and so far as the wine was concerned, it was seen that Canadian dockers were as addicted to pilferage as stevedores anywhere. But they were more efficient at it, and casks were broached and their contents transferred to water canisters with stylish secrecy, and no docker was ever found drunk on board. Mr Gregan turned an understandably blind eye to their predations, for they were the hardest workers we had come across. The wine seemed to act like fuel, and the ship was unloaded in record time. A cargo for the home trip was loaded with the same brisk competence at nearby New Westminster on the Fraser River, which was then a solid mass of wriggling salmon struggling pell-mell in a headlong flight to the sea.

For a dreary week there was salmon on the menu twice daily: then we were following their kindred into the straits, and veering south to the tropics for the last time, away from a land of misty mountains and rain-wreathed forests that reminded me of the country to which I was returning.

When we passed San Francisco I thought of Scotland again, for there lived Uncle Tom who had emigrated from Fife many years before. And then it was my turn to think of family, and I wondered how my father was coping with his retirement and a homebound routine. He had sailed the China seas when they were infested with pirate junks; he had seen pre-war Shanghai and Peking, and sailed up the Amazon to primitive places. He had lived in the United States in the prohibition era, waiting on a ship after the Wall Street collapse. Twice his ships had been torpedoed, and once he had drifted in an open boat for days in seas torn by winter gales. Was it likely such a man could settle down to the meek observance of Edinburgh's staid social customs? Now he had swallowed the hook, he would have to stay in one place, be biddable and conform. I foresaw problems of adjustment.

And how would my mother cope with him? Searching in my heart for the truth of these things, I started to question whether I was wise in proposing to embark on a new career at all. Would it not be simpler for me to float around this fascinating world, caring nothing for the future and leaving my worries in the last port, as seamen say? Who knew what dangerous or challenging situations were in store, what romances I should become involved with, as my ship sailed from one unknown land to another: the excitement of not knowing what lay ahead, and the door to adventure always open. . . .

23

Quandary

The *Rembrandt* began the long run down to Panama, hugging the coast, and as the distance home lessened, my anxieties about the future increased. I could not decide what to do, and I changed my plans as often as my socks, which was frequent when sailing past Mexico, for the heat was unbearable. The coolest place in the ship was the stokehold. Riley, as an experiment, fried an egg on the metal deck, and remarked that the flying fish must sizzle when they returned to the sea. Jagged coastal mountains wavered in the air currents as though they were melting. When we were not scratching at prickly heat rashes, we stood inert and panted like dogs. Notions of rain obsessively occupied our minds.

The heat didn't help to clarify my dilemma, and a more serious distraction had come to invade my thoughts. This took the form of wild vacillations of mood, ranging from suicidal despair at life's apparent meaninglessness, to peaks of sudden exaltation in which all things seemed to be engaged on a vast, mysterious enterprise. At less extreme moments I was aware of an aloof self-satisfaction, when for instance I had completed a difficult poem, but shortly afterwards at a harsh word or a fancied slight I would be thrown into a fit of dejection. I was given to arguing aggressively on abstract issues, such as history, politics and even philosophy. It mattered little that I had acquired my sparse knowledge of these subjects by gobbling large chunks from the chief's library, since my victims were selected on the assumption that they would be more ignorant of them than myself. My arguments were not wholly spontaneous, for I took the precaution of discussing them beforehand with

Wainwright, with whom I had become friendly. He belonged to the best type of Englishman, was reserved but affable, modest though self-assured, and without a trace of chauvinism. What drew me to him particularly was his extensive knowledge of the ancient world. He intended in fact to resume reading archaeology at Oxford in the autumn, and this was to be his last trip.

In the cooler parts of the day we would pace the foredeck while I regurgitated the material of my haphazard reading; and with unobtrusive tact, he would correct my misconceptions, hint at superseded theories, and generally attempt to improve my understanding of things ancient and modern. When the lunch- or dinner-gong rang I was primed and ready for action against anyone rash enough to engage me in argument. I must have been irritating company, and it never occurred to me that the phase I was going through was the manifest sign of an internal distress.

At Balboa, in Panama, we held a party to celebrate the birthday of Mr Travis, the permanently drowsy second mate. No one who was present may wish to remember that night but I shan't forget it, for it was then that my torment of indecision reached a climax.

The evening started like any other. After dinner the stewards cleared away the dishes to make room for the bottles and cigars, and shortly the oak-panelled saloon with its gleaming brassware was filled with an agreeable air of anticipation and conviviality. The Rembrandt reproductions gazed down at us with their familiar blend of mystery and intimacy; the grizzled tramp under his incongruous golden helmet, and Hendrikje, the artist's model, leaning patiently on one elbow, from her bed-closet. They had become dear to me in a way I couldn't define, and I felt a pang of regret that soon I should never see them again in this setting; likewise the men gathered round the tables with whom for the most part I had been on friendly terms. Everything would change after this trip, whether I left the sea or not. Captain Davis, looking pinker than ever, was to become a company superintendent, a shore-based job, and the corpulent Mr Gregan would take his place. Minto, who seemed incredibly handsome in the glow of the lamplight, was going to nautical college for the second mate's certificate; Wainwright to university for his degree. A demobilization system operated then, and most of the crew had fulfilled their obligations to their country. They could make a fresh start ashore, if they so wished, and Riley and Purdie intended doing just that, the one in the shipyards of Belfast, the other at Glasgow Art School. Only the older officers would remain at sea, having nowhere else to go.

As the drinks circulated, and cigar-smoke wavered in the air, it crossed my mind that this was a nodal point in all our lives; not only a birthday party but a premature farewell gathering which could never be repeated, for, once docked at Hull, we would take off for home as soon as possible, disperse and scatter into the waiting future with hardly a backward glance at the old *Rembrandt* whose existence had brought us together. And from that same future would come new men to fill our roles, and the ship would sail off as before, like an agent of destiny. Momentarily I viewed life as an infinite tapestry of co-ordinated scenes constantly changing and overlapping, dissolving and reforming endlessly without apparent plan or purpose yet leaving in its wake sufficient clues for me to guess at an immense and intricate scheme which was perhaps nearing a stage of completion.

To free my mind from this chilling picture I concentrated on Mr Thorpe, who was recounting a curious tale about the early history of the Panama Canal; but even so my attention wandered. In any case I had heard his story before, yet my imagination was triggered by its references and, as he spoke, I recalled the excitement of approaching the isthmus and nosing into the canal, stepping up through the locks to the wide Gatun Lake whose mangrove fringes concealed alligators, or so Riley said: now we were entering the long stretch that led to Balboa and passing *en route* place-names conned at dull school lessons – Darien, Gamboa, the Kalibra Cut. . . . Then we were descending through the Miraflores Locks to sea-level and the Atlantic was right ahead! It was as if geography had come dramatically alive. In the space of a few hours we had sailed barely fifty miles through a canal which linked two oceans and split a continent in two. According the the chief engineer, when the canal was due to be opened worried newspaper readers warned the editors that since one ocean was four feet above the other, the consequences of joining the two would be a cataclysmic flood as the higher sea flowed into the lower, and this would create an eccentricity in the world's rotation sufficient to dislodge the planet from its orbit round the sun. The company was silent as it contemplated the spectacle of mother earth slowly departing from the solar family and careering forlornly into galactic space, like a dying wolf limping into the long night of a wintry tundra. And all because a few politicians and engineers had combined to solve a problem.

The credulity and conservatism of people were discussed, and the mentality of those who held that when God made man the custodian of the earth it was only on the understanding that it wasn't to be tampered with in any way.

'There are still some folk who believe the world is flat, sure there are,' said Riley. 'Christian fundamentalists, for instance.' His Northern Irish brogue made the term sound like a swearword. I noticed his hair was thinning and his face prematurely lined, and I wondered if he too was going through a crisis.

'Well, gentlemen,' said the captain, 'I think at the end of this trip we can offer them some proof to the contrary.'

I still marvelled at this, that when we reached Hull we should have circumnavigated the globe.

'As a matter of fact, sir,' said Wainwright, 'proof has been available since Heraclides demonstrated in the fourth century BC that the earth rotates round an axis. And later, Eratosthenes used trig to measure its circumference. But it was Posidonius the Stoic who used a different method and arrived at the figure of twenty-four thousand miles – about three hundred miles from its actual size. Of course they measured in stadia, not miles.'

'Seamen must always have known the world was round,' remarked Mr Travis. 'Coastal cliffs are seen before the shore-line in clear conditions. But the distance is the same.'

He was right. Often at the wheel I had seen a liner's masts appear above the horizon before its superstructure. In those perfect atmospheric conditions only the sea's surface curvature could explain the truncation.

'Then why, Sparks,' I asked, 'with so much evidence that the world was round, did people persist in their mistaken assumption?'

'Mariners don't influence prevailing schools of philosophy,' he said. 'Then Greek thought declined, the Romans weren't so intellectually adventurous, and the great fire of the Alexandrian library destroyed most of the work of the ancient geometers . . .'

'Admit it, Wainwright,' Riley cut in harshly, 'a spherical

world didn't fit in wit' the teachin's o' the Christian Fathers!'

'True, they had some responsibility for the step backwards. But after the fire, there was a period of confusion out of which came the transition from Graeco-Roman polytheism to the monotheism of the early Christians. And by then a round earth didn't accord with their world-view, so to speak.'

'But how could they have a "world-view" when they knew so little of the world?' asked Purdie.

'Well, they were knitting together a system of beliefs which attempted to explain everything. They could hardly leave out the shape of the world, even if they got it wrong. Besides, they were mainly concerned about our preparedness for the next world.'

Riley laughed sarcastically. 'You mean by offering us pie-in-the-sky-when-you-die?'

'Who knows, Mr Riley,' said the captain, rising. 'There may be nourishment there of some kind, even to satisfy your sceptical palate. If you get there, that is.' Nodding to the mate, who also got to his feet, he withdrew with him amid respectful laughter.

The company relaxed and glasses were topped up before conversation resumed. Wainwright led off. 'You'll be pleased to learn, Riley,' he said, 'the Greeks discovered that the earth and the planets revolved round the sun, and this knowledge too was suppressed by the Church, even after Galileo rediscovered it.'

'The Church!' muttered Riley. 'It would have been better if Christ had stuck to his lathe. All that organized mumbo-jumbo to a god who, if he exists, must be sick to death wit' the lot o' them!'

'As for the existence of God, Riley,' said Mr Thorpe, 'the Greeks had no doubts on the matter. And they too believed that life was a preparation for death and the soul would be judged on its past behaviour. Is that not so, Wainwright?'

'More or less. But Socrates thought that only philosophers would pass muster when it came to posthumous judgement. According to Plato's Phaedo, that is. Herodotus is less positive.'

The talk passed on to the Platonic ideal, the theory that everything had its divine counterpart in an adjacent but invisible world which was the real one, the world of form.

It may have been the effects of a third glass of rum and Coca Cola, but I suspected a flaw in the theory. 'What about that

trading schooner we saw in the Hawaiis? There was some cloud
about, but the sea was like glass and reflected a perfect
mirror-image of the ship. Has the reflection an ideal form?'

'No, precisely because it was a reflection. It was twice
removed from its heavenly prototype,' replied Wainwright.

'Then what about the clouds? How can you have an ideal
cloud when it's always changing its shape?' I asked, rather
smugly.

'Jock's got a point, Wainwright,' said Travis. 'What's more, if
all things have a perfect version of themselves in this abstract
universe of yours, then there must be an ideal concentration
camp, an ideal torture chamber, and an ideal atom bomb. All of
which strikes me as somewhat less than heavenly.'

Wainwright laughed. 'I didn't invent the theory, old man.
Nor do I support it, but my own pet stumbling-block concerns
the evolution of species, and the Greeks didn't know much
about that.'

I thought I understood his difficulty: the differences between
some species and others were so approximate that only experts
could detect them. So why should heaven need so many
variations? And where would it find room for all the prototypes?
There were a quarter of a million types of beetle alone.

Then I saw I had a captive audience, and a heaven-sent
opportunity to air a theory of evolution I had been considering
for months. The time and place at least were ideal, and the
company seemed to be in an indulgent mood. It went thus:
since nature is a constant source of energy continually expressing itself through evolving forms, man would have to adjust to
its pressures in order to survive; and the only aspect of his
composition capable of progressive adjustment was the mind,
with its own driving force of the *Will*. The mind was the matrix,
the Will its fertilizer. Therefore man could transcend himself. . . .

I gave them the gist of it, and they looked doubtful, as well
they might; then Purdie said: 'He could . . . but will he *Will*?'

The chief snorted. 'Superman stuff! He's been at my Nietz-
sche.'

'The main problem lies in finding a way of altering the mind
that is benign, for both the individual and his society,' said
Wainwright. 'And I don't see how it could be achieved without
turning the world into a laboratory. People wouldn't like that.'

'But the natural world is a laboratory,' I retorted. 'There have been plenty of failed experiments, from the dinosaurs onwards. And we may be the next, if we don't learn to alter our basic attitudes to things like religion and acquisitiveness, and war. The last one hasn't been over for long, and already the Americans and Russians are squaring up to each other...' – I slurped my drink and ignored a dig in the ribs from Minto – '... each side supremely convinced that their cause alone is right. That's how it's always been, with the Romans, the Spaniards, the French, and the British Empire.'

But I had gone too far, upsetting an applecart.

'Steady on, Jock!'

'Superficial twaddle! As if you could compare our empire with...'

'It's true!' I said, nearly shouting. 'Every major power attributes its greatness to the special favour shown to it by God or Mahomet or whatever tribal deity it has adopted...'

'Karl Marx?' interposed Purdie with a grin.

'... which entitles them, as by historic inevitability, to conquer yet more countries by an assumption of divine approval. As if any supernatural omniscience would give tuppence for their absurd pretensions, their flags and massed bands.'

'You're on the morning watch, Jock,' muttered Minto, trying to bring me down to earth.

But I hadn't finished.

'The fact is, that man is a loner, like the shark, but he needs to be gregarious to survive. And these conflicting characteristics have split his mind, and religion has compounded the fracture. But unless he learns to heal himself, we're done for, and we'll join the mastodon and the sabre-toothed tiger in museums of natural history. Stuffed!'

There was a good-natured uproar at this, which matched the tumult in my excited brain, but my knees wobbled as I got up and allowed Minto to lead me from the saloon. On deck I drank in lungfuls of air and noticed that the stars were vacillating like my knees. My last thoughts before a drunken sleep overtook me was that I should take up modern history, maybe even politics.

Next day on the foredeck Wainwright said: 'You were in good form, last night, Jock. You're wasted at sea. Go to university and get these random ideas of yours into some sort of order.'

'But I love the sea!'

'You won't always love the sea, old man.'

We went in for lunch. The lime-juice never tasted better and I felt calmer than I had been for weeks. The way was now clearer.

24

Jamaica Rum

Just before sunrise we picked up the pilot and steamed gently into the bay, an unblemished sheen of water reflecting palms by the shore, the velvety green bush, a huddle of rusty roofs that was Port Royal, and a decrepit jetty where we would tie up for coal. The ridge of the Blue Mountains was feathered in gold.

'Slow ahead . . . easy port,' said the pilot, sleepily.

'Slow ahead,' replied the mate, pulling back the telegraph.

The harsh sound of the bell was an affront to the tranquil scene. A barracuda, like a pencil of light, broke the surface, trailing a wake of silver chevrons.

'Easy port,' I said, giving the wheel a half-turn till the bows lumbered round towards the little town and the jetty. A longshoreman rose stiffly, stretched long arms above his head.

'Steady . . . steady as she goes. Stop engines,' said the pilot.

'Steady . . . steady as she goes,' I answered, easing to starboard briefly to check the weigh. The mate oscillated the telegraph rapidly, signalling 'finished with engines'. A touch to port, then starboard, and I had her true on course, 15,000 tons of ship and cargo gliding smoothly to the rickety pier.

Jonesy up for'ard bent a line on the hawser's eye and threw the bight to the longshoreman who drew up the hawser and dropped the eye over a bollard. Down aft Spiers whirled his line cowboy fashion and sent it spinning to the quayside. Both hawsers were winched up and back-springs made fast. We had moored safely.

I sighed with a mixture of pride and relief, for there is always some risk of collision steering a vessel into port. The pilot smiled approvingly, and the mate's nod of dismissal was less curt than usual which, from him, amounted to a compliment; so I took advantage of our improved relationship.

'All right if I take the day off, Mr Gregan?'

His small eyes darkened with suspicion, and I knew he was thinking of Fiji and New Zealand, and possibly other misdemeanours.

'I promise not to stray too far, this time . . .'

'You'd better not. The ship leaves at eight bells tonight, and we won't wait for you. Don't go into Kingston, by the way . . .'

'Right, sir. Thank you,' I said, prepared to agree to anything so long as I could explore some of this beautiful island. But first I would post my letters, to the company and my parents, for my doubts were at an end.

Minto was on the morning watch but the bosun's squad had opened the hatches and there was nothing for him to do; so we dressed in our tropical kit and after breakfast made our way ashore with a few Canadian dollars in our pockets. I found a post-box and, holding my breath, dropped the letters in, and sealed my fate.

We went for a swim from a nearby strand, surely the original of subsequent vermouth advertisements, with its yellow sand, palms and delectable mountains.

'You're going to miss all this,' puffed Minto doing a backstroke. Then a black fin cleaved the water, found a gap in the shark-barrier and cruised into the cordoned-off area.

'I won't miss the sharks!' I yelled, and we raced ashore.

From the beach we saw the fin was attached to nothing more lethal than a playful dolphin. It was time for a cooling drink.

We dressed and wandered into Port Royal, a jumble of shabby colonial buildings grouped round a square of beaten earth on which ill-clad children played games with pebbles and scrawny curs sprawled panting in the shade.

'There's a café!' said Minto, pointing to a balconied house with garish signs announcing the sale of American soft drinks.

Dazed already by the heat, we were glad to step into its dark, cavernous interior. From instinct we chose a table near the door. A barefoot Jamaican girl detached herself from the shadows, her smile weary with experience.

'Coca Cola,' said Minto. 'And sarsaparilla for my friend.'

Other figures emerged into focus and padded to our table.

'You English? You buy us drinks.'

'I'm Scottish,' I said. 'My friend's English, but we've no money.'

'Come on. You plenty dollars. You buy us rum.'

There were about four of them, all barefooted, loose of build and slack-breasted, and all on the far side of forty.

'You buy drinks, yes?'

'Sorry, but as we explained . . .'

'Hey, Jacko . . . these men no wanna buy drinks!'

A tall, gangly person, a panama hat hiding his eyes, sidled in view. 'Why you no buy drink for Lucia, eh?' he said. 'She nice girl. They all nice girls. Why you come here if you no wanna buy drinks, eh?' And he leant his bony hands on the table.

Minto was easily aroused, and I had seen him floor a man much less menacing than Jacko; but there were the women. . . . 'We did come to buy drinks, but not for your friends,' he said, 'and we still haven't got them. So we'll go elsewhere.' And he tried to push past the man, at the same time giving me a significant glance. Two years ago I wouldn't have known what it meant. Now I did: we were in a brothel.

'So!' said Jacko. 'You don' like our girls, eh? Fine talk. Where you find better, you tell me?' And he tapped Minto on the chest.

It was a rash move, for Minto swung at him, connecting nicely with the man's dark jaw and sending him crashing into the tables.

In a moment the women were on us like a pack of harpies and we were darting out to the square, fending them off as best we could, the walls echoing with their cries and shrieks. Rounding a corner that led to the main road, we ran into a party of soldiers climbing into an army truck, and the women dropped back.

'Want a lift into town, mates?' shouted the driver, sizing up the situation.

We accepted readily and piled in the back of the truck with the others. The women laughed heartily as we took off.

'Where are you bound for?' asked Minto, still panting.

'Kingston, of course. It isn't far.'

I thought it best not to mention the mate's embargo on Kingston, so only one of us would be in trouble if he should find out.

We passed a side-road leading to the jetty where the *Rembrandt* was taking on coal, then the road swung away and she vanished out of sight, and there was a view across a bay to

Spanish Town, haunt of pirates in the old days. The sea was intensely blue and I felt stirred, already aware of a precocious nostalgia. When would I sail such waters again?

'You see that fort on the hill,' said a sergeant. 'Built by Henry Morgan, it was. Once they'd made him Governor.'

'Captain Morgan, the pirate?' I asked.

'Yes, mate. The navy couldn't beat him, so the government got him on our side. Poacher turned gamekeeper, you might say.'

Above a cluster of trees we saw crenellated walls, and glinting cannons trained towards what had once been the Spanish Main; then we were rolling past colonial bungalows and down the streets of Kingston to the docks, where we took our leave of the friendly soldiers. Before they left, they advised us that a naval launch departed from there to Port Royal at six-thirty in the evening. That left plenty of time for us to stroll around this elegant town, its squares and gardens, the colourful markets filled with gaudily dressed Jamaicans, and the more sedate areas which bore an unmistakable stamp of Englishness, with bowling-green, tennis club and cricket field. Everywhere trees and shrubs shouted with brilliant blossoms, oleanders, bougain-villaea, and the vividly scarlet poinsettia. At the end of each street there was a view of green hills, dazzling sea and moored white ships. In that respect it was like any tropic town though cleaner than most; but there was a difference, for I was seeing it with senses sharpened by an anticipated regret. I was saying goodbye to all the tropic places I had seen, as well any immediate prospect of seeing others.

Minto may have shared this mood, or it may have been the heat and the lazy ambience of the place, for we were suddenly caught off-guard. Coming from a restaurant after a late lunch, we were surrounded by a gang of youths. They were more threatening than violent, but it was clear that, if we offered resistance, there would be a fracas and we should get the worst of it. So for the second time that day we retreated with more haste than dignity while the youths hurled stones and insults, and what sounded like political slogans. As we raced along a thoroughfare we saw the tennis club and hurried through its gates as though entering a sanctuary, and our pursuers gave up the chase.

'You chaps look pretty hot, I must say,' said a portly figure in white ducks from the clubhouse veranda. 'Better have a drink. . . . Steward!' He removed a topi from a chair, and we sat down.

We apologized for the intrusion and explained what had happened. He clucked his tongue in sympathy and stroked his moustache. 'Happens a lot these days, I'm afraid. It's all this fellow Bustamante's doing, you know. He was a convicted killer and we threw him in gaol. Pity we didn't hang the blighter, but he was set free for political reasons, and now he's stirring up the hotheads. Shouldn't be surprised if he became Governor some day.'

'Like Captain Morgan?' I asked. 'Poacher turned gamekeeper?'

'Not quite. Morgan was useful to us, in the end. But Bustamante won't be satisfied with anything less than total independence, mark my words. And the island will go to the dogs!'

My contentiousness had largely disappeared, since I had resolved to go to university, so I held my tongue. And it would have been tactless and ill-mannered to point out that what he really meant was that Jamaica would become intolerable as a refuge for retired British colonels. In the meantime we were grateful just to be there, sipping iced drinks and watching tanned colonials playing tennis while the system which made their graceful existence possible was cracking under the strain of tensions they were unwilling to understand.

Younger members were introduced, and they shared the colonel's opinion; but in general, it was bad form to talk politics. They knew that subversive elements were trying to rock the boat, but their attitude resembled the old ladies who heard burglars downstairs: if they didn't make a sound, maybe they would go away.

The afternoon slipped by agreeably till we remembered the launch. A horse and trap were summoned and we were driven to the harbour just as the launch was casting off. We daren't miss this boat, and Minto and I leapt from the quay together, landing on the stern of the small craft, and causing the bows to rear like a porpoise and the Royal Navy crew to swear at us like bargees.

At Port Royal we disembarked and hurried to the *Rembrandt* close on eight bells. Everything seemed in readiness for departure; hatches were battened down and derricks housed, but it was rare for both the captain and the mate to be at the gangway's head. Something was up, for they were on the verge of apoplexy.

'Where the hell have you two been?' bawled Mr Gregan, and without waiting for a reply he explained the situation. Most of the crew had gone on the spree in town and were drunk beyond reason. Unless we brought them back, we couldn't raise steam, so the ship would miss the tide and the company would be charged extra harbour dues.

A small rescue party was put under our control and we led it back to the house with the soft drinks signs, for where else would they be?

Inside, pandemonium reigned. It was like a scene from Dante's *Inferno* prinked up with a dash of mayhem. The harpies of the morning were petrified, and Jacko was not to be seen. Half-naked seamen lay under tables or sprawled over them, dead to the world. Those still on their feet teetered round the floor with glazed expressions, while others at the tables leant back in their chairs singing their heads off, occasionally crashing to the floor. A gramophone playing a calypso added to the din until someone heaved a bottle at it and the music screeched to a halt. The singing grew louder, then split into two rival groups each trying to outdo the other. Some of them recognized us.

'Bless you for being an angel . . . just when it seemed that . . .'

'So I snapped my fingers ya-ha-ha-ha! No pirate could be bolder . . .'

'There's Minto! And Jock! Come an' have a drink, boys!'

It had been a long day: we should need fortification for this assignment, so we tried a little. There was no doubt of it, the rum was a glorious liquid, rich, mellifluous and treacherous. And the men had sold everything but their denim trousers to get their hands on the stuff, even their shoes.

We made a start on the drunks under the tables, and the women who had been wailing in the background like a Greek chorus, came to our aid. Soon there was a regular procession of bodies being carried or dragged back to the jetty. The bosun had swung out the davits of the centre hatch and a cargo tray had been lowered to the quay. One by one the inert figures were piled on the tray like logs then winched aboard and dumped on the hatch, where the bosun played the hose on them while we returned for another load. The café girls were now our allies, since they were as anxious as we were to transport the unruly seamen to the ship.

However, in the town other locals had gathered to jeer at the white man in difficulties. I obliged: the denims of a lanky trimmer I was carrying became entangled with his trailing feet, and gradually the denims slipped down, to a crescendo of glee from the bystanders. I dropped the naked man and wished myself a thousand miles away when, to my amazement, some girls came forward and shyly replaced the trousers, and then helped me carry him to the ship. Soon they were part of the team, and like all Jamaicans they lightened their work with song:

> 'Drinking rum and Cocaah-cola . . .
> Working for the Yankee dollaah!'

When the last of the drunks were aboard, the engineers had bullied the first batch down below to put a pitch on, and we cast off at midnight. When I came off watch four hours later, Jamaica lay astern against an embroidery of stars, while the sky paled over the Caribbean towards Cuba and Haiti, names tinged with romance and mystery.

The *Rembrandt* was bound for Hull.

25

Hurricane

Five days out from Port Royal the weather changed and something happened to the sea we hadn't seen before. A wayward swell arose, the surface went rip, and the sky was heavy and brooding. The wind started to keen, a high, wailing sound, something between the cry of an anguished soul and an air-raid siren. We sensed that massive forces were mustering, flexing giant sinews before the assault. The glass fell rapidly.

There were sudden vicious portents of this strength: like a cat toying with its prey, delaying the kill to make the moment sweeter, the sea would grip the vessel and fling it sideways, hurtling sleepers from their bunks and crockery from tables. An uneasy peace would follow, until the next surprise attack. Older hands noted with slight satisfaction that the deck cargo was stacked to the levels of the poop and fo'c'sle head, so forming an unbroken line of superstructure, and this would deflect some of the weight of the overtaking storm. The deck cargo, therefore, was bowsed up more securely, canvas hoods lashed over the cowls, and vents turned away from the wind.

In time a blanket of churning cloud lowered over the rising sea like jaws snapping shut on a helpless quarry, and the waters were covered with a luminous darkness that was like the end of the world. For a week there was neither day nor night, and men groped and stumbled about their tasks in this demoniac twilight in which winds screamed unceasingly and monstrous waves advanced, rose and fell in terrible succession.

Early in the gale there was a potent sign that this would be no ordinary storm. At four bells on the evening watch I had battled my way aft to read the log. The ship was bucking and writhing like something gone mad and I gripped the taffrail for dear life. As I stood there squinting through the gloom and spindrift at the log-dial, something made me look up to the towering seas looming above the port quarter: and there, leaping from the wave-crests, and higher than our mastheads, came school after school of big fish – porpoises, dolphins, tuna and marlins, and other species unknown to me, all launching themselves from the lee-side of the clifflike waves in untidy unison and, like our ship, carried along by forces neither of us could withstand. Men and fish were powerless against the ocean's wrath, but the fish were being driven from home waters while the *Rembrandt*, though reeling and shuddering from every massive deluge, was borne relentlessly towards our own.

Then under the shrieking wind and the noisy tumult of the sea, and, as the stern reared, the rattling race of the screw, I heard a new sound, one that I never expect to hear again. It was like a deep, vibrant sigh, and I peered over the side from which it came and, hardly believing my senses, saw, not twenty yards off, a mature sperm whale, also running before the storm. For a long moment its black, gleaming eye, as big as a dinner-plate, stared into mine. The creature gave another profound sigh as water shot through its blow-hole, then the great boxlike head sank under the next wave. I gaped after it marvelling, hoping it would reappear and indifferent to the seas surging about my waist.

On the third evening I was on fo'c'sle look-out, firmly wedged between a windlass drum and a gunwhale buttress, when four bells rang out, a reminder to check the lights. Quitting the comparative safety of my position, I crossed to each side to make sure all was well with the ship's lights. Starboard and port winked back reassuringly, and the foremast light glinted dully. But I couldn't see a glimmer from the mainmast truck, which was about twenty feet above the other. I tried climbing on the windlass for a better view, but a wave dashed me to the deck just as Jonesy, who was on farmer, emerged from the darkness with a mug of cocoa. He could have spared himself the trouble, for another foaming cascade descended on us and I thought the man was overboard. But the bows lunged up and there was Jonesy, a dripping cone of oilskins and clutching the companionway rails as though he would never leave them. I pulled my way towards him and bawled: 'The mainmast light's gone! Tell the mate!'

Jonesy had the sort of face which, whatever his emotion or the circumstances, always broke into a smile. Even as the deck shifted grotesquely under our feet and a new wave tumbled down on us I guessed it was still in place, impervious to the fury of the Atlantic. But his souwester swivelled round to stare aft through the rigging of the heeling masts and falling spray, and I saw it nod in confirmation.

It was useless trying to shout a warning to the bridge in that howling wind, so, gripping Jonesy's shoulder, I gestured that he should report the news to the mate without delay. Just then a huge wall of sea broke over the bows, engulfing everything and wrapping us round the windlass, which we grabbed with desperate tenacity.

It was now a matter of urgency that Mr Gregan should be informed, for the SS *Rembrandt* deprived of a mainmast light was reduced to the status of a trawler, and we were approaching the main shipping lines between North America and Great Britain. Without seeing a juxtaposition of masthead lights, no vessel in the vicinity could estimate our direction of travel. Article 29 of the Regulations for preventing collision at sea made no bones about it: 'Nothing in these rules shall exonerate any vessel, or the owner, or crew thereof, from the consequences of any neglect to carry lights or signals. . . .'

Meanwhile, it was impossible to keep a look-out in those atrocious conditions, so I decided to leave the fo'c'sle and explain to the mate how things stood. No doubt a Royal Navy midshipman would be cashiered for deserting his post; and the same Article 29 contained a warning about failing to 'keep a proper look-out'. I had to suppose the Merchant Navy was more flexible about its rules, for I preferred to leave the service on my own terms and not be thrust out with ignominy.

Jonesy had entwined his limbs into the gear of the windlass, like a child clinging to its mother in a thunderstorm. It ought to have made me suspicious. Firmly taking his arm I motioned to the bridge and helped him to his feet. Together we stumbled down the companionway, drenched through despite our oilskins, and staggered amidships under the lee of the deck cargo.

Entering the wheelhouse, I said: 'Can't see a thing from the fo'c'sle, Mr Gregan. And the mainmast light isn't showing.'

'Get Spiers up here, and he can keep a look-out from the monkey island,' ordered the mate promptly. Then: 'Know where the bulbs are stored? And where to find the switch-box?'

I nodded, knowing where both were to be found. What was not certain was who would be chosen for the job. My stomach tightened in a knot of panic at the thought of going up the mast. Often I had been up to the yard-arm to take photographs of the ship, but that was only half-way up, and never in a force thirteen gale.

'It's against regulations for you to up, Green. You're under-age. Take Jones as far as the yard-arm. He'll do the rest.'

I tried not to show my relief and hurried down to the galley where Jonesy was shivering over the stove and grumbling to Spiers. I gave Spiers his instructions, then, with Jonesy in tow, went to the alleyway where the switchboard controls were located and turned off the current. From the engine-room we obtained pincers and the correct bulb for the job, which was as big as a coconut. Thus equipped we made our way to the mainmast, the decks now constantly awash, and stared through the spray and darkness at the crazily swinging masthead some eighty feet above the deck. A metal ladder was clamped to the mast up to the yard-arm. The light-bracket was fixed to the cross-trees near the truck, and this was approached by a wire-rope ladder attached between the yard-arm and the masthead. It was barely visible from the deck.

'After you, Jock!' yelled Jonesy with his usual grin.

I hooked an arm round the rung of the ladder, opened my oilskins and tucked the bulb under my sweater. I had thrust the pincers into my knife sheath. I buttoned up and began the long climb to the yard-arm, making sure Jonesy was following.

The ship was heeling erratically about twenty-five degrees on either side of the vertical. This meant that, the higher we climbed the greater was the arc of radius as we swung from port to starboard, and at the extremities of the swing the broiling seas leapt up like fantastic tentacles. It was better not to look down.

The sounds of sea and wind were deafening, but when we reached the yard-arm there was a different kind of noise altogether. Alarmed, we peered upwards and saw the wire-rope ladder clang against the swinging mast with a fearful whiplike motion. *Crack* ... the ladder struck the hollow mast, the sound

echoing with a dull boom. Somehow it had to be scaled, and as I
tugged the light-bulb free I wondered how Jonesy would tackle
the problem. I held out the bulb to the man, my spare hand
clutching the small rail that surrounded the yard-arm. To my
horror he waved his hand dismissively, and his sou'wester
wagged from side to side. 'You won't get me up there, Jock!' he
cried above the wind.

Crack went the ladder again. The ship lurched sickeningly and
we were thrown on to the rail. At that moment I knew stark
fear.

'I can't do it Jonesy,' I shouted. 'It's against regulations.' I
tried another tack: 'If your shipmates hear of this, you'll never
live it down, and you won't get another ship!'

'I'm not going up that ladder!' he repeated, and I could swear
I saw the man grin, evidently a sign of nerves. He was as scared
as I was and preferred to lose his reputation rather than his
life. I couldn't blame him, but the ship was in jeopardy and
there might not be time to go below and fetch Spiers.

All at once the ship veered lopsidedly at the mercy of a rogue
seventh wave, and far below the decks disappeared under a
confused torrent of sea. When she straightened up, I thought I
saw something where the horizon used to be, a brief fan-shaped
flicker of light.... Maybe the mind was playing tricks, but I
could use it as a bluff.

'Ship to port, Jonesy!' I yelled. 'If there's a collision, men will
drown and you'll go to gaol, if you don't go down with them.'

He shook his head again. It enraged me. I called him all the
crude names I could think of, then, telling him to grip the ladder
tightly against the mast, I tucked the bulb under my sweater
again and began the most difficult climb of my life. Each time
the ship heeled, I was hurled at the mast as though by a
catapult, but in time I learnt to catch the impact on shoulder and
thigh, so preventing the bulb shattering into my stomach. Soon
I was making better progress, and the cold lessened the pain of
bruised limbs and hands chafed from the wire rungs. It seemed
to go on for ever, jabbing one foot after another on the rungs as
the mast swayed ever more widely over a chaos of seas; so I was
surprised when I reached the lamp bracket, and with stunned
senses I stared at the curved glass as though wondering what I
was doing there. Almost automatically, I locked my legs into the
wire rungs to free my hands, then eased out the pincers and

unscrewed the wing-nuts. I removed the dead bulb and flung it into the darkness, screwed the new one in its place and clamped up the glass. The job was done, and I scrambled down the swaying ladder to the yard-arm aware for the first time that sweat was coursing down my face.

I ignored Jonesy and slid down the steel ladder to the deck. Supposing the bulb is a dud? I thought, as I waded to the alleyway. But when the current was switched on, and I returned to the deck, the light shone out clearly through the spindrift from the masthead. Whether there was a ship in the offing I shall never know, but if there were, she would have no difficulty in judging our direction of travel.

Eight bells rang out, signalling the end of the watch. There was no need to go back to the bridge, for Spiers would report 'Lights are bright' from monkey island; and Gregan might ask awkward questions about my bleeding hands. So that was the end of the matter. Maybe Jonesy wouldn't grin quite so much in future, but his secret was safe. And I was grateful to him, for the experience showed that anger can overcome fear, and necessity tap unsuspected resources.

The following day the gale worsened, or perhaps we were nearing the eye of the storm, for no one could remember such a havoc of seas, a blind, devastating rage of the elements. It was a period of limbo. Clothes were never dry, sleep was impossible, and regular hot meals a distant memory. Mind and senses became dulled, though a measure of alertness was essential and made the difference between life and death as the seething decks pitched and heaved under slithering seaboots.

There was no conversation. Functional instructions were conveyed with economy and carried out with dogged competence. Ordinary relationships dissolved; there were only the outlines of men lurching and stumbling down alleyways, across decks to the saloon, the galley or the bridge. The edges of reality were blurred. Two men were needed to control the wheel, which fought under their grasp like a crazed demon.

Perhaps purgatory would be a better description of that time; yet when look-out was transferred to monkey island, the highest point of the superstructure, there were glimpses of sublimity. As I sheltered behind the canvas wind-break, wrapped in oilskins, there was something in the awful majesty of the scene that filled me with indescribable exultation. As the ship rose high on a wave-crest the view opened out to range after mighty range of towering waves advancing towards the *Rembrandt* as though their sole purpose was her destruction. Then she would lurch into a trough and a hill-like wave would loom above, seeming to pause as if to take aim, then crash thunderingly down on the decks of the capering vessel.

There was an occasion when the entire ship except for masts and funnel was submerged under a toppling seventh-seventh wave, and for an eerie moment I felt like the sole survivor of a wreck alone on a raft in mountainous seas. The ship had literally sunk beneath my feet, and in that howling wilderness of waters, not knowing if I should ever see ship or crew again, I knew the ultimate degree of loneliness and desolation.

Possibly no more than twenty seconds elapsed before the bridge and the blunt cowls of the vents appeared, and the rearing fo'c'sle head; then the ship was shaking herself like a black retriever that had clambered from a pool, and we were being buoyed up on another crest and the innumerable ranges were still advancing 'as terrible as an army with banners', though no metaphor is adequate to describe the spectacle. It was an awesome pageant, an irresistible procession of natural power that reduced the concept of self to a cipher. Yet strange as it seems, it made me think of the rolling interwoven phrases of a Bach organ fugue, a profound climax of experience that was like an expression of the occult *will* of the universe itself, or maybe a reminder of the chaos from which all things originated.

It seemed I had stared into the face of the oldest of gods and had heard his music. After this, I thought in my ignorance, nothing that life throws at me could be of much significance; for I had seen the fundamental terror and grandeur of things, an elemental dynamic that lay beyond the scope of all philosophy and theology. My petty concerns shrank to nothingness, and I saw no reason why the demands of the world of men with their trivial goals could ever diminish the revelation I had seen in the heart of a hurricane. . . . Ignorance indeed.

26

Fog Ahead

On the seventh day we had rest of a sort. The billows were still swollen but they had lost their murderous intent and we could walk the decks without being swept off our feet. Winds were low and racing, and still plucked spume from the crests, but for a few hours daily a wan light filtered though the clouds. The worst was over, it was time to inspect the damage. This was surprisingly slight: the lanterns to the men's quarters were smashed, and mess-rooms and cabins had been flooded throughout the storm. The awning spars had been ripped away and their steel stanchions were buckled beyond repair; but the general opinion was that the deck cargo had saved the ship.

At last sunlight broke through. It was like a benison, and with the Gulf Stream and the westerlies helping us along, the ship seemed to be charged with a sudden vitality, like a hard-driven mount scenting the stable. No longer were spells at the wheel like agonizing wrestling matches: instead a half-turn this way or that could maintain the course in the constant sea, and the helmsman could dream of home.

The *Rembrandt* was spruced up. Squeegees were vigorously applied to decks encrusted with salt, lifeboats and davits were painted, and the bridge lining varnished. It was a means of showing affection for the ship which had carried us safely through the storm, and men sang at their tasks. As the weather brightened, they gathered on the after-deck in the evening, to crack jokes, overhaul their gear, and sing songs to the accompaniment of Shepheard's wheezy melodeon. The scissors of amateur barbers glinted in the sun. A sequence of flaring sunsets closed those last days, staining the wake with crimson and pearl, as though the elements were trying to make amends for their previous ferocity.

A new camaraderie was noticeable, and old enmities were forgotten. Friends, who would part for ever at Hull, swore to keep in touch and exchanged addresses. The bosun's sarcasm became playful, almost mellow, and Mr Gregan took to humming quietly to himself on the bridge. In the saloon Purdie and Riley chatted amicably together and discussed the rival merits of Belfast and Glasgow without quarrelling. When we gathered in the chief's room for pre-prandial drinks, the conversation was less concerned with history and politics than theatres and concert halls we intended to patronize in our home towns.

There was an explanation for all this: the crew were in the grip of 'the Channels', that humanizing fever which affects the toughest of seamen as his ship approaches the old country from the south. Again, the men down aft talked fondly of their families, and many must have regretted the presents they had bought for wives and sweethearts but had bestowed instead on the café girls of Port Royal in return for rum and other services.

I had my own family preoccupations, but I couldn't confide them to anyone, not even Minto. The first interview with my parents would be awkward, to say the least. My mother would be reproachful, my father querulous. I imagined it would go something like this:

Mother: But we thought you liked the sea?

Self: I loved it, and I still do.

Father: Then why the blazes are you quitting?

Self: I want to do something creative.

Mother: What, for instance?

Self: I'm not sure yet. Maybe architecture or civil engineering. Or perhaps English literature or natural history.

Father: I can see you've given the matter a lot of thought. And how are you going to live while you make up your mind?

That would be the tricky one, for they would be in no mood to subsidize a new career. I should have to get a job to earn fees for a university crammer school. The prospect of becoming even a temporary clerk was not enchanting, and I wondered how I would adjust to a nine-to-five routine in a drab office after two years circling the world in a tramp steamer. I almost envied Minto, whose life was mapped out, and, like himself, clear-cut.

Next month he would enter nautical college and study for the second mate's certificate. He had 'fixed things up' with Dorothy, she of the Spanish costume, and some day they would marry, buy a house in Kent and raise children. He would make an excellent officer and probably a good father. His wild oats sown, he would settle easily into his chosen role, his career would advance steadily and usefully, and his life would have the aspect of a seamless garment, rounded and complete. But for me, there was a missing ingredient about such a life. It was too bland, and it begged a question. If life had a purpose, it must involve growth and development, maybe as an expression of evolutionary dynamics. Minto's male offspring could repeat his life exactly and no one would complain, least of all the politicians and tax-gatherers. But in the long term nothing would be added to the world, its enigmas would remain and their challenges be ignored. There was no reason why Minto shouldn't ignore them; but at the end of his successful life one might ask, in the rather portentous words of Yeats: ' What then, sang Plato's ghost?'

I suspected that my way through life would be more intricate than Minto's, and that I might grieve my parents before I had steadied on course. They would not at first appreciate my compulsion to discover what lay inside of myself, or my need to explore the ungeographical world and relate it to the apparent one. They would see me as a stranger, taller and stronger than when I left, and with political notions they might not admire: but they would not know me as I was now. And how much did I truly know of them? Breaking my indentures with the company would sadden them, but their concern might be no more than a display of conventional disappointment. In their deepest hearts they could not be too upset, for my father must know the problems of a seaman's life; and my mother must have wept countless times at their prolonged separations. Surely she would not want me to impose that on a future wife?

Not that I would mention such things, any more than I could suggest to my father that as a senior officer I should be exposed to risks of alcoholism. We had carried a deck officer, for a while, who had been demoted from the position of captain on a prestigious liner because of drink. One night he jumped overboard in a fit of delirium tremens. When his loss was discovered we circled the area but he was never seen again.

However, I couldn't use that story in my defence, not to my father. It was against the rules, like hitting below the belt, and I too was conventional. Or I had been conventional until I met Selima and Sheila and a dozen other girls; until I had raided the cargo for sacramental wine in Tasmania; until I had violated several regulations and laws both civil and maritime, culminating in my being hunted as a wanted man by the New Zealand police.

There was another matter I should have to consider. At sea my transgressions were accepted as ordinary behaviour, except by the captain and the mate who were supposed to be *in loco parentis*. And they, like parents, referred to a morality which was not always acknowledged in their personal lives but was thought to be useful in curbing the volatile waywardness of youth. Once settled at home, I should have to do without the cheerful tolerance of shipboard mores and subject myself to the demure staidness of Edinburgh's social life. How should I cope? The period of readjustment might be painful. My transition to an acceptance of the ways of seamen had been gradual; the step back would be abrupt.

That difficult step would have to be taken if my hazy plans were to be realized. Then one gusty afternoon it came appreciably nearer when a strip of mist on the horizon appeared on the port bow, separating the racing, marbled sea from a cloudless sky. Behind the mist lay Land's End and The Lizard, and much else besides: we had learnt from home of the bureaucracy there, of the ration books and prefab houses, the worried men in demob suits queuing in dreary lines at labour exchanges for a pittance, or the chance of wage-slavery in post-war Britain. No one could blame Dusty Millar, Bill the Donkeyman, Brownlee and Griffiths and a dozen others for turning their backs on it all and playing dice with fortune in new countries where they would not be hedged in by rules, governed by petty officials, tabulated and indexed as mere units in an impersonal system. And Chippy Hollins could never retrieve the equivalent of his anchor and cable in that emaciated land beyond the mist.

The course was altered to east-nor'-east. The gulls found us and came swinging out on the beat of the wind, crying and swooping for scraps thrown by the galley-boy. Yesterday we had seen the last of the dolphins, and we died a little as they wheeled south, leapfrogging the waves towards the sun and lands of Cockaigne, to palmy isles and climates of turquoise and gold.

The way to our more austere destination became less distinct as the mist swelled out from the land and towards evening thickened to a spreading fog that covered the sea and the ships travelling our way, obscuring the stars overhead. We slackened speed in accordance with regulations, and sounded two blasts on the fog-horn at prescribed intervals. Through the night this melancholy note continued like a lost soul in mourning for itself. By noon of the following day the fog was impenetrable off the Isle of Wight and the engines were reduced to dead slow.

It was like a nightmare from which I never expected to waken, as fog-horns, far or near, sounded their deep, plaintive calls from all around. Now to port and growing stronger, then to starboard but with no diminution of volume; and sometimes right ahead so that collision seemed inevitable. And all the while other ships approaching the Solent or bearing westwards were converging on the area, each adding her own throbbing groan of despair from a changing position until the thick torpid vapour, which enveloped us like a shroud, resounded with a muffled cacophony that was like a crazed orchestra from the depths of hell.

There are many forms of fear, but I know of none quite like the nauseating panic that gripped me then, for I was sure the ship would go down with all hands. How pathetic, I thought, if I should die just as I was preparing to launch myself into the actual life of the world. There were so many things I wanted to do, ill-defined though they were; but whatever they might be, they would be real and true to myself, unlike the romantic notions which had tantalized my mind when I was at school, maybe gazing through a classroom window on a hot summer's day while a master droned on about the Corn Laws or the causes of the Industrial Revolution. I might be thinking of a recent letter from my father telling of exotic foreign lands, of 'far-away places with strange-sounding names', and a desperate longing to sail to the ends of the earth would seize me like a passion. Now I had done just that, and I could cite a few bizarre names of my own to conjure with: Kalamata, Lourenço, Marques, Tel Aviv, Wooloomooloo, Vanua Levu, and plenty of others. I didn't need any more. My nautical appointment, I saw now, had been a means to an end, and the end had been achieved.

It may be that times would come when I should regret my decision; that whenever a certain spring wind blew across the hills at home, it would awaken more than buds and seeds from their winter sleep, and I should be impatient to tear up roots and sign on as a deckhand in any old rusty tramp with a south-bound charter and feel a heaving deck under my feet again, and see spindrift glittering over the bows ploughing through a dazzle of seas, the rigging arcing out and singing in the salt-tasting breeze. It was a risk I should have to accept, but I was convinced that the annual yearning would lose its strength when I knew what it was I had to do. 'Happy the man who has found his work,' said Carlyle. I must find mine. For the present it was concealed by a different fog from that which surrounded the SS *Rembrandt* as she crawled blindly along the coast, rounded South Foreland and made her tortuous way to Hull. But I knew it was there, as surely as a familiar but darkened room makes known the presence of its furniture. I should have to brace myself for a few barked shins.

And when I had discovered that work and I had practised it to the full, then and only then would I be content to make the last voyage of all, set sail, and say with an easy mind, Whither O Ship?